YOU'RE GROUNDED FOR LIFE

Misguided Parenting Strategies
That Sounded Good at the Time

TIM JONES

ISBN: 978-1-4834-4354-6 (sc)
ISBN: 978-1-4834-4355-3 (e)

Lulu Publishing Services rev. date: 2/3/2016

Contents

Critical Praise for *You're Grounded for Life—Misguided Parenting Strategies That Sounded Good at the Time*

"If you're looking for really funny social commentary and clever, thought-provoking insights into this experience we call parenting, all I can say after reading this book is... keep looking." – Deanna Martin, Dallas Evening Star Telegram

"There may be well over 50,000 books on parenting, but in my humble opinion, this book by Tim Jones is undoubtedly among the top 49,500—give or take." – Ed Morrison, Pacific Press News Service

"Before I read Tim Jones' book on parenting, I thought most parenting books were just boring, wordy treatises where the writer simply pontificated on how they are an expert without giving any practical, helpful advice whatsoever. But then I read this book. I stand by my previous comment." – Lee Runnells, Harper Conrad Publishing

"'Brilliant,' 'clever,' 'playful,' 'insightful,' 'informative' and 'helpful' are all words that immediately come to mind when you ask me to list random adjectives with more than one syllable." – Maria Hernandez, English Teacher, Crestview Middle School

"At least this book was something to keep him occupied and out of trouble. God knows he's not qualified to do much of anything else in this world." – Betty Jones (the author's mother)

"Tim Jones' book *You're Grounded for Life - Misguided Parenting Strategies That Sounded Good at The Time*—What do I think of it? Well, if that's not a train wreck waiting to happen, I don't know what is." – Frank Nash, the author's High School English teacher

"Can you get off the computer, Dad? You've been hogging it all day. And besides, nobody is really going to read any of this crap anyway." – Rachel Jones, author's daughter

"This book is 100% recyclable and biodegradable!" – Ned Witherspoon, Spokesperson, Department of Conservation, Portland, Oregon

"Can you tell me how to get to the Space Needle?" – Melvin Turnblad, a Seattle tourist whose quote we accidentally placed in this book but did not catch our mistake until after the book went to press

"I can't believe how incredibly, unbelievably awful this drivel is. I sure hope he doesn't give up his day job. I mean, it's really horrible." (<u>Note to self</u>: Be sure not to use this quote. This guy really seems to hate me.) – Charlie Mann, Portland Beacon Herald Sun Times Post-Gazette Dispatch

"I can't speak for his writing ability, but to be honest, he sucks at racquetball. Is it okay to say 'sucks'?" – Keith Weinberger, racquetball partner

About the Author, Tim Jones

Tim Jones is perhaps the most brilliant humor writer since Mark Twain. I know that's pretty high praise, but since the person typing this "About the Author" section is Tim Jones himself, he pretty much gets to say whatever he wants. And we simply don't have the budget to hire fact checkers every time Tim puts in writing some outrageous claim which might not be 100% factual. Tim also invented the Internet, not to mention the modern combustion engine and early prototypes of the first central air conditioning system. Oh, and the Clapper. He invented that, too. Tim is currently working on a device that turns urine into 100% safe, potable water but has not been successful in getting any of his friends to test the efficacy of his invention. Tim also wrote the lyrics for the viral hit song *Gangnam Style* (in the original Korean).

After Tim served two terms as the United States Ambassador to the United Nations, he started humor writing. He writes a weekly humor blog called **View from the Bleachers** (www. ViewFromTheBleachers.net), which is read by hundreds of millions of people on every continent. He is particularly loved by Norwegians, for reasons unclear, even though ironically, Tim does not particularly care for Norwegians (but he refuses to explain why). Okay, perhaps that was a slight exaggeration about hundreds of millions of readers everywhere. Let's just say his total readership is somewhere between 12 and 9,000,000 readers. Even more if you include the Internet Spammers who routinely post comments to his articles, like this actual recent quip from one of his anonymous fans: *"Am not sure where you're getting your info, but great topic. I needs spend some time learning much more. Thanks for excellent info I was looking for this."* The praise does not get much better than that, does it?

Tim writes about a wide variety of issues from parenting to politics to the latest trends in lifestyles—often with nearly perfect punctuation and grammar. Not long ago, Tim was privileged to join the ranks of a very exclusive club. The A.A.R.P. invited him to become

one of their very first 80 million elite members. In order to be considered for membership in this exclusive society, one must be over 50 years of age, have a pulse, and go to the bathroom on average at least twice a night. Tim is honored to say he was accepted after only his third application for admission.

Tim is based in Camano Island, WA, a lovely island whose residents were delighted to welcome him to their ranks—until they started reading his weekly humor blog. He is currently on probationary status with the other island residents. In his spare time, Tim plays tennis, golf, racquetball and other sports—none of which he will ever come close to mastering. He is also married to a talented portrait artist and is the father of two wonderful girls he and his wife adopted from China as infants. Without them, this book absolutely would not have been possible.

Dedication

Author's daughters Emily (top) and Rachel enjoying the snow back when they actually enjoyed hanging out with each other.

I dedicate this book to my amazingly wonderful daughters, Rachel and Emily, without whose endless persistence in attempting to ingest dangerous objects as toddlers, refusing to keep their room clean as teenagers, and a litany of other devious efforts to do everything in their power to push their father to the brink of emotional exhaustion over the past twenty years, this book would not have been possible. I can't imagine what my life would have been like these past twenty years without both of you in it. And sorry about the 15,000 times I told you, "Remember, make good choices." I imagine that got pretty old after a while. I will always love you to the universe and back.

I further want to dedicate this book to my incredibly patient wife, Michele, who in addition to being an amazing mother to our

daughters, has somehow managed to put up with the harsh reality of sharing her life for the past 28 years with a husband who has the emotional maturity of a 15-year-old and who considers fine dining to be any meal where either peanut butter or sharp cheddar cheese is served. She is the love of my life, my best friend, and as I said on our wedding day, I want to grow old with you.

I consider myself blessed to have a family that puts up with my sophomoric sense of humor and is actually willing to be seen in public with me (well, so long as I don't attempt to hold hands).

Acknowledgements

I want to acknowledge two incredibly talented people, without whose critical contributions this book would not have been possible. In other words, if you've already read this book, are ruing the fact you just wasted several hours of your time and are wishing you could have those precious hours back, then these two people are partly to blame. I'm talking about my editor, **Betsy Jones**, and my graphic designer, **Holly Koziol**.

Betsy Jones, in addition to editing this book, has been my co-conspirator for the past several years helping me on a weekly basis with my humor blog, <u>View from the Bleachers</u>, attempting (sometimes in vain) to take what I write and turn it into something coherent. Sadly for her sake, Betsy happens to be distantly related to the author of this book—and by distantly related I mean she's my sister. While I have tried repeatedly to convince her that all my spelling, punctuation and grammatical errors have been deliberately placed for humorous effect, she refuses to buy any of my lame excuses.

Betsy patiently waded through every article of this book, searching desperately for ways to turn what I have composed into something vaguely intelligible, and if possible, figuring out a way to reveal glimmers of humor. ~~Betsy is really an incredibly talented person who, I have found over time, to have an enormous gift for being able to take what I write and pare it down to the key points for maximum impact and communication effectiveness.~~ *[Tim, way too wordy. Try this instead: Betsy is a masterful editor. – Betsy]* See what I mean? You're the best, Betsy.

Tied with Betsy for being the best is my amazing graphic designer, Holly Koziol. I have collaborated with Holly for several years on other projects, and I knew when it came time to produce this book, she was the only person I would trust to create a visual presentation that would bring these articles to life. I can't say enough about Holly's outstanding creative ability and impeccable design

skills. Besides, if I go on much more about how talented Holly is, it will probably just piss off my other collaborator, Betsy. I wouldn't want to work with any other graphic designer on this project than Holly. Besides, the other ten people I approached to design this book all refused to be paid in "Free Hug" coupons, so Holly was my only hope.

I also want to acknowledge the contributions of the following talented people: Taylor Swift, Matthew McConaughey, LeBron James, Kim Kardashian, Kanye West, Jennifer Lawrence, Stephen Colbert, George Clooney, Rihanna, and Donald Trump. That's because I did a Google search just now on the "top ten most Googled celebrities" and their names came up. I figure that mentioning them in my book might improve my book's search engine results.

Finally, I want to thank Chipotle for everything they did to help get this book published. They are in my humble opinion simply the finest fast food restaurant in the world and are making the world a better place through their philanthropic efforts in every city they have a restaurant. I just can't get enough of their crispy corn tacos. Okay, so technically Chipotle had absolutely nothing to do with this book. I was just thinking that by giving them a plug, they might send me a gift certificate for "Free Chipotle Meals for Life." Hey, it could happen. This is America—the land where dreams come true.

Introduction

This book is for any parent who loves their children, wants to make the world a better place, has hope that there may someday be a cure for cancer, cares about the environment, or loves America (or if you're not American, then whatever country you call home—except for Belgium—this book is NOT intended for Belgians. Sorry).

But if you hate children, want to make the world a worse place, have no interest in a cure for cancer, hate the environment or hate America, this book is definitely not for you—unless you have enough money for the cover price of this book and want to purchase it anyway, in which case this book is absolutely for you, too.

Outside of my immediate family, I am widely recognized as a parenting expert. I have been a parent of two girls for over twenty years—and for many of those years, there were long stretches—sometimes lasting days at a time—during which neither of my children thought I was the world's worst dad. Oh sure, I've made my share of parenting mistakes along the way. My idea to have our kids find jobs to pay for their pre-school tuition was probably not the best, in part because they kept getting turned down for employment due to being too young to read. (Age discrimination against toddlers is something that I have long opposed.)

As a result of some of my parental missteps over time, I realized that being a good parent is not all about just giving your kids expensive presents—although it doesn't hurt if you're trying to score popularity points with your teenager. No, being a good parent is about tolerance and patience. Lots and lots of patience. I mean endless frickin' patience. I don't think you quite understand. I'm talking about *"I still love you even though you flushed my Rolex down the toilet"* levels of patience.

Being a good parent also means putting the needs of your kids ahead of your own desires. (Unless your team is on Monday Night Football, in which case, the kids can fend for themselves. A man

has to have boundaries.) I decided to write this book to help other people who may be just starting out on this journey called parenthood, to avoid making some of the mistakes I made. For example, never tell your younger daughter that she is prettier than your older daughter. It turns out that even if you say, *"Now this is just between you and me. You can't ever tell your sister I said so,"* it really doesn't seem to help. Young children don't quite grasp the concept of *"Don't tell mommy I blew $200 at the track"* either.

I have divided this book into four chapters: Early Childhood, The Teenage Years, and Off to College. Okay, technically that makes three chapters. I added a fourth chapter to cover additional special strategies that won't fit into my chronological approach to this book. Deal with it.

I hope you will enjoy this book. I don't claim to have all the answers to parenting. Just most of them. But over the past twenty plus years of parenting two daughters from diapers to diplomas, I can tell you with conviction that I have keen insights and understanding into the minds of most kids and adults—just so long as those kids and adults are not female.

Thank you for reading this book. And if you like this book, please consider subscribing to my weekly humor blog, View from the Bleachers (www.ViewFromTheBleachers.net). Like this book, my humor blog contains absolutely no calories and no trans fats. And that's a commitment to my readers I never intend to break.

CHAPTER ONE

Early Childhood—Or "Oh, Dear. What Have I Spawned?"

"Don't worry, your father won't notice."

Warning Signs You May Be Experiencing Kronic Incessant Disorder Syndrome (KIDS)

Over the past 50 years, throughout North America, there has been an explosion of reported cases of **K**ronic **I**ncessant **D**isorder **S**yndrome (better known as KIDS). No socio-demographic group has been spared this invasive and intractable outbreak. In fact, I myself have been waging my own personal battle with KIDS for the past 20 years.

According to humanitarian relief agencies' longitudinal studies dating back to the 19th century, the number of known cases of KIDS is at its highest level in human history. Alarmingly, it shows no signs of reversing its upward trend. For millions of couples facing the long-term ordeal of KIDS, there is no relief in sight.

This woman has just learned she is yet another victim of KIDS. While there are many effective methods of prevention, as of today, sadly, there is no known cure.

Scientists have been unable to unlock the mysterious inner workings of KIDS. But they do know that contracting the condition has been conclusively linked to unprotected sexual contact, often during bouts of excessive alcohol consumption. Warning signs that you may have contracted KIDS include an inability to maintain an orderly household, often accompanied by a sudden indifference to the presence of vomit, nasal mucous, or fecal or urinary discharge on one's clothes or person.

What makes this epidemic of KIDS so debilitating is that there is very little anyone can do to combat it. Once contracted, in the vast majority of cases, the condition, while not usually fatal, typically lasts a lifetime. People coping with even the mildest form of KIDS report that the condition gets progressively more difficult to manage over time, as the virus mutates in appearance, continually

grows in size, and in later stages becomes increasingly resistant to attempts to control it. As people struggle to adapt to living with KIDS, they report that close friends they've known for years but who have not contracted KIDS often avoid them like the plague.

Early stage KIDS is often associated with significant sleep deprivation lasting up to two years. During this "incubator" period, common side effects include a significant decline in the victim's range of vocabulary, typically accompanied by an uncontrollable urge to speak in a high-pitched chirpy voice about successful bowel movements.

Scientists have identified an alarming phenomenon in people suffering with KIDS—a noticeable deterioration in their mental faculties. They speculate that this intellectual impairment may be caused by prolonged exposure to vacuous television programming dedicated to letters of the alphabet or endless recitations of drippy songs about Baby Belugas or beautiful days in the neighborhood.

Surprisingly, after a few years, some KIDS sufferers have reported brief intervals of partially regained lucidity and fleeting episodes where the worst aspects of KIDS appear to go into in remission. They can sometimes regain normal sleep cycles and are able to enjoy more adult-themed TV programming. There have even been reported instances in which people living with KIDS have experienced momentary fits of laughter at birthday parties, zoos, and little league games—but these anecdotal stories have yet to be substantiated with empirical evidence.

One of the most common ailments afflicting people with KIDS is a perceived loss of control, independence and spontaneity. Sufferers often report feeling chained to endless cycles of vehicular transport to soccer games, piano recitals, and doctor's appointments, taking the place of time previously used for hiking with friends, playing tennis, and working out at the gym. As a result of this hard-to-break cycle, another common side effect of KIDS is unsightly weight gain and a marked decline in concern for personal appearance.

It is common for people with advanced stages of KIDS to experience wild swings of emotion and increased levels of stress. If you encounter an otherwise rational adult barking out phrases like *Who do you think paid for that?* or *Would it kill you to say 'Thank you'?* or *Because I said so!*, the chances are high the person is battling KIDS. Adults exposed to KIDS for long periods of time often suffer a dramatic depletion of their long-term savings. Some studies suggest this steep decline in personal net worth intensifies around the 18th through 22nd year of living with KIDS.

The good news is that there are glimmers of hope. For some people facing an uphill struggle with KIDS, symptoms of frustration and exhaustion tend to fade about the time the financial strain of managing KIDS has passed its peak. There are dozens of documented cases where victims of KIDS can resume relatively normal lives somewhere around 18 years from the onset of the condition, engaging in conversations about politics or professional sports teams, or taking long drives that no longer require emergency pit stops to eliminate bodily fluids—unless you have tangentially contracted OABS (Overactive Bladder Syndrome), which can afflict KIDS sufferers in later stages.

While there are several effective methods for the prevention of KIDS, currently there is no cure. The unsettling reality is that the existence of KIDS has become a global epidemic. Ever since my wife and I first received the shocking diagnosis 18 years ago that we had both become exposed to KIDS, our lives have been consumed just trying to manage this condition.

But here is the oddest part about this crisis. Even though coming down with KIDS has radically turned my life upside down, drained my life savings and caused me endless worry, I can't help but wonder what my life would have been like if I had never gotten KIDS. For me, KIDS is one lifelong condition for which I don't want to find a cure.

Always Lie to Your Kids

I love my kids. That's why, when they were young, I made a point to lie to them every chance I could. As any experienced parent knows, you need to lie to your young, impressionable children to help prepare them for their lives as adults—and to help you forge a trusting relationship.

Parents who care about their young children start lying to them early in their formative development—ideally while still in the womb. Don't wait until they're in middle school. By then your chronic pattern of honest communication will likely have caused irreparable damage.

There are many reasons we adults lie to each other: to get out of cleaning the garage despite your wife's incessant nagging; to deny that you scarfed down the last piece of your wife's birthday cake; or maybe to hide the fact that you were really golfing when I, er, I mean *you*, told the wife you were helping a buddy move. Of course, there are also bad reasons for lying, but at the moment, they escape me.

But when it comes to children, caring parents know that lying is a way to avoid crushing their kids' self-esteem. It's not your job to destroy your child's hopes and dreams by dispelling the myths of their childhood. That's their future therapist's responsibility. Your job is to keep telling your kids whatever you need to, to get them to behave, brush their teeth and maybe, just maybe, not kill the family cat, Bonkers.

The following is a list of important lies you must tell your kids with conviction so they don't grow up to be as socially awkward and emotionally insecure as say, well, their father.

Santa Claus is real. While he does appear to bear a striking resemblance to Uncle Harry, that's just a coincidence. It can't be Uncle Harry, because Harry is usually plastered at some dive bar on Christmas Eve, bitching about how his ex-wife took him to the cleaners in the divorce.

I love your latest piece of artwork. Oh, I totally get how it's a painting of me. You totally captured my essence. You are so talented. I really like how you painted me with a toaster on my head—or is it a palm tree? And what's with the five arms coming out of my ears? Or are those bananas? Either way, it's totally me. Well done, my little Picasso!

I can't believe how great you are at T-ball *(or soccer or running or maybe just standing still and not falling over)*. So you say you were the last child picked to be on a team? I'm sure they picked you last because they were just trying to be polite to the other team. Who wouldn't want my little superstar on their side? I noticed that you almost hit the ball off the T-ball stand today. You're getting so close, kid. You know, this is how Babe Ruth started, I'm pretty sure.

I had so much fun playing house today. I can't believe those three hours went by so fast. How many servings of pretend tea would you say you poured me? I'm guessing 127, but I lost count after 75. And thank you so much for the invisible cookies you served. They were

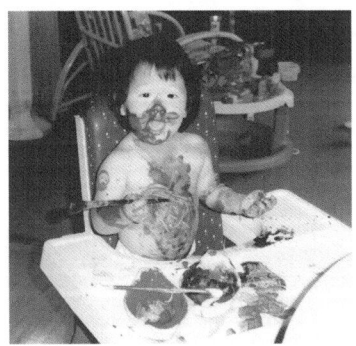

scrumptious. Hey, just a suggestion: Maybe next time how about we try playing house without dressing Daddy up as Little Bo Peep? I would hate to spill any of the pretend jam on the lovely bonnet you made me wear. Thanks, Angel.

No, your mommy and daddy were not fighting. Why would you think that? We always raise our voices when telling each other funny stories. When you heard Mommy shout, *"I've had it, doing all the damn housework. Go take*

Check out our daughter's SELF-PORTRAIT. I lied and praised her artistic impressionist masterpiece. Clearly inspired by Picasso – NOT!

a hike!" she was just suggesting we stop working and go out for a fun hike somewhere—separately. And when I yelled back, *"Well, screw you!"* I was simply asking Mommy if she had found that screw I was looking for. Your Mommy is so good at finding things.

Mm-mmm good. That sure was a fantastic breakfast you made for Daddy. You really did an amazing job of mixing together so many ingredients that have never been combined before—by any human being. How did you think of adding the chocolate sauce and onions to my Lucky Charms? You're so creative. And I don't think I've ever seen frozen waffles prepared that way before. Were the gummy bears your idea? Brilliant move to skip the step about thawing out the waffles first. I can't believe how full I am after just two bites! Yummy!

You were great in the school Christmas play. And to think they cast you as the fifth Christmas tree from the left—the star of the show. I was so impressed by the way you stood there the entire time and never moved...and never spoke...or did anything else. Just like a real Christmas tree. I am so sorry that I could not stay for the entire two-hour performance. But I got a call from the President of the United States. He needed my help with a top secret matter to save the country. The President says he's sorry he missed your Christmas tree performance.

So be sure to lie to your young kids every chance you get. After all, before you know it, they'll be all grown up with young kids of their own to lie to. And you don't want to be the one to tell your grandkids that Santa Claus is really Uncle Harry, do you? I didn't think so.

Oh, one more thing. Before I forget, can I just tell you that you are my absolute favorite reader of all? Honest.

Kids, Ask Me about God –
By Reverend Tornquist

I am privileged to feature a LIVE CHAT with noted Christian evangelist Reverend Norman Tornquist, host of the popular webcast, *Kids, Ask Me about God*. Tornquist is the renowned author of children's books including *God Loves Kids with Braces Too*, and *Skittles—The Devil's Gateway Snack*. We join the LIVE CHAT already in progress....

Reverend Tornquist: I see we have a question from Sophie. Hello, Sophie.

Sophie: Hi, Reverend Toadkiss. I'm four years old. I love toads!

Tornquist: That's *Tornquist*. An understandable mistake.

Sophie: Whatever. I wanted to know—Is God left-handed like me?

Christian scholar Rev. Norman Tornquist tackles kids' questions, like *In Heaven, do I still have to eat my peas?* And *Will my daddy get all his hair back when he meets Jesus?*

Tornquist: What an interesting question, Sophie. I really don't know. I will have to pray about that one.

Sophie: So what you're saying is you know nothing about God. How did you ever get to become a priest?

Tornquist: Actually, Sophie, I'm not a priest. I'm a minister. I see that Billy has a question. Go ahead, Billy.

Billy: Hey, Cardinal Tornquist

Tornquist: Actually it's *Reverend* Tornquist, Billy. What's your question about God?

Billy: I want to know, where does God go to the bathroom?

Tornquist: Another fascinating question. Thank you, Billy. Well, God is all-powerful. So, I guess he can go to the bathroom anywhere he wants. When it rains in the forest, maybe that's God's way of peeing.

Billy: Wow, I had no idea God had to pee so much. Maybe he has a tiny bladder. Sure hope my parents never make me go on any more camping trips. I never knew how gross the outdoors was. Thanks, Cardinal T.

Tornquist: It's Reverend...Never mind. Let's take another question, shall we? I see Angel has a question. What a lovely name, Angel. Do you have wings?

Angel: Not anymore. My mommy took away my angel costume because I threw her cell phone in the poopy seat. She's still mad at me for that.

Tornquist: I am sorry to hear that. What's your question, Angel?

Angel: Well, Reverend Tornquitter—

Tornquist: That's *Tornquist*. I am not a quitter. Go ahead with your question, Angel.

Angel: Ok. Last night I overheard my mommy in the bedroom shouting "Oh, God!" and "Yes, Yes, Yes" over and over. Do you think my mommy was talking to God last night?

Tornquist: Um, in a way, maybe. Maybe God was coaching your mommy and daddy on how to make a baby.

Angel: My daddy was out of town last night. But his brother was here. Do you think mommy and Uncle Carl were trying to make a baby for daddy? Yippee! Maybe I'll get a baby brother. Can I name him Eddy, after my guppy?

Tornquist: Um ...er...um.... Let's hear from James. What's your question?

James: Hi, Mr. Thorn-squished. I want to know why they gave Jesus a timeout up on that pole. Was he being naughty? Did he talk back to his daddy or something?

Tornquist: That's *Reverend Torn*...oh forget it. Well, James. Jesus was not being naughty. He was dying for our sins. His father loved him very much.

James: His daddy sure had a strange way of showing it, if you ask me. When my daddy tells me he loves me, he usually buys me ice cream. He would never give me a timeout on a pole.

Tornquist: Did you know that Jesus's father is God? God loved Jesus very much—just like he loves you.

James: Uh oh. Does that mean he's going to give *me* a timeout on a pole, too?

Tornquist: Not to worry, James. I think you're safe. I see we have a question from Tony.

Tony: Hi! My kitty cat Patches died yesterday. I am very sad. Will Patches go to Heaven even after peeing on the carpet?

Tornquist: I am sure Patches will go to Kitty Heaven. She is in a good place now.

Tony: Oh no! God turned Patches into *a girl?!!!?* This is the worstest thing ever. He was such a great boy kitty. And now God turned him into a girl? How come? Is God going to turn me into a girl when I die?

Tornquist: No, Tony, he's not going to—

Tony: First God puts his boy on a pole and now he turns my kitty into a girl. I don't think I like God very much. He's a very mean man.

Tornquist: Um, he's actually very nice. Trust me. Let's take another question. How about Anna. What would you like to know about God?

Anna: Last week my daddy ran a stop sign and smashed into another car. The other driver got out of his car and started screaming at my daddy. He yelled, *"Jesus Christ. Didn't you see the God-damned stop sign?"* My question is this: Is my daddy really Jesus?

Tornquist: I don't think your dad is Jesus.

Anna: Are you sure? Because I think it would be really fun if my daddy was Jesus. Can you ask God? But tell him my daddy is sorry about the accident so that God doesn't give him another timeout on a pole, okay?

Tornquist: I'll put in a word for your dad, Anna. Thanks. I think we have time for one more question. It comes from Harold. Go ahead, Harold. What's your question about God?

Harold: Was Jesus a communist?

Tornquist: I'm sorry, Harold. Come again?

Harold: Was Jesus a Commie? Because he was always telling everybody to share their toys and their bread and stuff. My dad says Jesus was a Communist.

Tornquist: Well, Jesus taught us to share with others. Jesus said that we should look out for those who are less fortunate than ourselves. But I don't think that makes him a Commu—

Harold: Because my dad says that nobody should be dependent on handouts from others and that you should make it on your own in this world...

Tornquist: Yes, but—

Harold: My dad says that millions of Americans sit on their asses and expect the government to take care of them with welfare checks, and that before long, this country will become a crippled, dependent, socialized welfare state like 1930's Stalinist Russia, putting an end to free enterprise and personal responsibility.

Tornquist: I was just saying that Jesus taught us to share with the less fortunate. How old are you, Harold?

Harold: Six. I like turtles.

Tornquist: Very nice. Well, that's all the time we have this week for *Kids, Ask Me about God*. Remember, God loves you, even if you wear braces.

Look, Daddy! I Landed the Space Shuttle!

Isn't it wonderful that so many parents are realizing the wonderful learning experience that is **Bring your child to work day**? It's an opportunity for your child to learn what you do each day while they're at school ignoring their teachers and texting their BFF in the row behind them.

So I was thrilled to read about the caring dad who, as an air traffic controller at JFK, invited his eight-year-old son to take over the controls. Yes, he put his son in charge of guiding planes during take-off and landing procedures (I can't make this stuff up). What a swell dad. And by all accounts, other than the near crash of a minor non-commercial twin engine plane, which overran the runway, the lad's instructions were almost flawless. Hey, how do you learn without making a few mistakes?

The 'feel good' coverage of this wonderfully involved father made national news, and it seems the idea has spread like wildfire. All over the country stories are popping up of dads and moms taking the initiative for their children's education by bringing them to work. What a wonderful bonding opportunity. Here are just a few recent heart-warming stories:

This police officer is teaching her young son a valuable lesson: "Jimmy, confess to stealing the Oreos, and I'll try to get you a reduced sentence. Otherwise, I can't help you, buddy."

Rusty Hammersmith, a fire fighter from the Bronx, NY, responded to a three-alarm blaze with his 11-year old daughter Becky in tow. Becky sure was a fast learner. She even rescued a cute little tabby kitty named Buttons from the 5th story of a burning apartment building just seconds before the floor completely collapsed.

Nine people suffered serious burns but I am happy to say that little Buttons came through with nothing more than minor scratches and is doing swell. And Becky only suffered mild inhalation burns. What a trooper!

Darcy McAllister, an aspiring accountant for a fast-paced Silicon Valley software firm in the process of seeking urgently needed second-round financing, had a great day with her seven-year-old daughter Clarissa, showing her how to move some funny-sounding items called "liabilities" *(Clarissa could not pronounce that word— she kept saying "libabilies"—it was so darn cute)* off the books and onto an offshore shell corporation. Clarissa had tons of fun shredding stacks and stacks of papers with lots of numbers on them. She suffered only a minor paper cut.

Dr. Irving Feingold, a Miami cosmetic surgeon specializing in breast augmentation, was beaming with pride as his 15-year old son Benjamin asked to join his dad at work last week, offering to assist the patients in their recuperation. Afterward, Benjamin told his dad it was an awesome *hands-on* learning experience—although in hindsight, the lad may have been a tad too enthusiastic when he offered to manually inspect whether the breasts were in fact successfully augmented. Seems a couple patients complained—they must not have kids.

In Thurmond, West Virginia, 43-year veteran of the coal mines Shamus O 'Daugherty invited his ten-year-old son Sebastian to join him in a special **Miners with Minors Day.** Dad and son enjoyed a truly memorable trip 400 feet underground. Trapped for more than four hours with a dwindling oxygen supply, due to the collapse of their only escape shaft, Shamus and young Sebastian had more quality time together than they had experienced in ages, although later Sebastian decided black was not his color.

Recently a governor of a Midwestern state gave his 13-year-old son Chris a special pen, once given to the Governor by actor Charlton Heston, and invited Chris to veto a popular gun reform bill and a landmark gay rights legislation. The youth signed each

YOU'RE GROUNDED FOR LIFE

veto with *"I'm King of the World!"* Chris even inserted some pork into the legislation while the Governor was in the rest room, setting aside $11 million for a gnarly skate board park for his middle school—complete with grinding ramps, split rails, quarter pipes and an adjacent go kart track. The young Governor-for-a-Day said upon signing his law, *"Dude, it's so tight. My girlfriend Stephie is gonna freak....Oh, sh*t. My old man is coming back. Quick, where's that bill about tax breaks for small businesses?"*

Birmingham General's Chief of Surgery Dr. Reuben Weisberg is extremely careful when he brings his 15-year-old daughter Crystal to join him at the operating table. He never lets her remove any organs without the closest of supervision, and even then, only minor ones at that, like the pancreas or ovaries.

For too long, kids have been kept at arm's length from our lives as doctors, mail carriers, bank tellers, computer programmers and bomb detonation specialists. It's time we gave them the gift of learning what their dads and moms do for a living—firsthand. Oh sure, there will always be a few jobs that are a little too dangerous for our kids to help with:

- *"Sorry, Kirsten. As much as I'd love it if you joined me, I don't think you can help your daddy in the meth lab today. I love you, pumpkin...."* or

- *"Hey, Billy, I would love to take you with me with me to Fallujah as I sweep the town for Al Qaeda insurgents. But how about you stay here in the green zone, okay, little buddy?"*

But for the rest of us, what a wonderful teaching and bonding opportunity to bring you and your special child closer together.

And a personal note to Earl Wiggins, from Waukesha, Wisconsin, who does chain saw sculpture for a living. Thanks for your question, Earl. How about we just let your four-year-old Nathan **watch** the first time out, okay? Perhaps let him finger-paint the totem pole instead. Thanks for asking.

When it Comes to Our Kids, Winning Isn't Everything. Whining is....

For too long, parents have been pushing their kids way too hard by doing outrageous things like telling them they need good grades if they want to get into college or harping on them relentlessly to practice piano for 30 minutes a week if they want to improve their skills. Those parents are monsters!

When I was a kid playing on various sports teams, year after year, the ruthless message drilled into me was that if you want to win, you have to try hard. And maybe even practice. I internalized this misguided achievement message at an early age. Little did I realize the long-term crippling effect caused by the constant parental pressure to "do your best" as a child. Years later, the damage is evident, as I now have a good-paying job and live in a lovely home in a safe neighborhood. I've even overcome failures a time or two.

I have passed the torch and sent my kids to excellent schools with teachers and coaches who push them to do their best. When will this vicious cycle of perseverance and achievement end? In hindsight, I now realize that all this harsh talk about doing their best and applying themselves was actually undermining my kids' fragile sense of entitlement.

Finally, a sports league in Canada has gotten its priorities about kids and "winning" figured out. Not long ago, the Gloucester Dragons Recreational Soccer League of Ottawa, Canada came up with a new rule designed to protect children from the emotional scars of losing in sports. The rule? If a team wins a game by more than five goals, *that team loses by default.* The rule was designed to prevent blowout victories and to encourage good sportsmanship. Hats off to you, Gloucester Dragons Soccer League. Well done.

The results so far have been impressive. Now, whenever a team goes up by five goals, their players usually stop playing, walk off the field, and head over to the playground to climb on the monkey

bars in order to avoid accidentally scoring the losing goal. Now that's true sportsmanship.

I applaud the Canadians' efforts. Oh, sure, some people may criticize this new policy as yet further conclusive proof that the USA can beat the crap out of Canada anytime it wants. But I will ardently defend this enlightened new approach. Our kids' psyches are extremely fragile from the first 18 months of life until the time when they no longer need our emotional and financial support—typically around age 37.

We need to shelter our children from anything that might damage their self-esteem, such as losing 27 to 0 in a youth soccer match, as happened to nine-year-old Sarah Miller's team last weekend. Sarah is the goalie. Think of what such a devastating thumping might do to her self-confidence. The last thing little Sarah needs is

"An F on your spelling test? No Sponge Bob for you." Poor kid. Fortunately, her parents eventually caved, as usual.

to internalize that she is a terrible goalie. (Although, as an aside, I have to say, Sarah really sucks at goaltending. She has no business being allowed out of the stands. But please don't tell her parents I said that.)

As the Ottawa youth soccer league has taught us by its inspiring example, when it comes to our highly impressionable young children, life should not be about winning and losing, or showing up for practice, or getting cut from the baseball team just because little Jimmy can't seem to figure out that the pitcher's mound is not first base. Instead, our jobs as parents should be to protect our precocious angels from the real world that is waiting to beat them into submission.

That's why I've adopted a totally new parenting approach that focuses on preserving my kids' belief in their greatness, regardless of evidence to the contrary. In the past, if a teacher gave my child a D on an important math test, I'd probably have a serious chat with my kid and ask why she chose to stay up till 1am playing Candy Crush on her cell phone instead of studying for the test.

However, I realize that such an interrogation might harm my child's belief about her incredible brilliance. Now, if that same teacher were to give my daughter a D, I'd immediately berate the teacher for unfairly downgrading my child's score simply because she gave incorrect answers. After all, when it comes to what's right or wrong on a math text, who's to say what the real answer is to 12 minus 5? It's all so subjective. And I would be sure to praise my little princess on her outstanding choice of using a #2 pencil and remind her that she's still an A+ student in my book.

Childhood flies by so quickly. You will have plenty of time later on to awaken your kids to the reality that life does not always even up the score to make sure everyone's a winner. Let someone else teach them that the world does not owe them a six-figure income and a penthouse condo by age 25. Now is the time to remind your young superstar how special they are—even if they just tripped and did a face plant during a soccer game, and did so while only riding the bench.

So, this summer, if by some act of blatant favoritism your perfect son or daughter does not get picked to play on your neighborhood's Select soccer team, remember that your child is still incredibly gifted. It's not your child's fault that she skipped all the practices and couldn't be bothered to show up for tryouts. That just means she has more time to work on that perfect tan this summer. She's going to be a suntan superstar, I just know it.

Encourage Your Challenging Child— Through POSITIVE Parenting

If there is one thing I've learned as a parent, it's that in the end, your kids will crush your dreams, ignore your advice, join a biker gang, and blame you for everything.

But if there is a second thing I've learned, it's that you need to be positive. As you know, outside of my immediate family, I am considered a parenting expert. My latest book, *A Positive Parent's Guide to Loving Your Child, Even If They're an Evil, Twisted, Unmotivated, Narcissistic Demon Seed Hellion Who Will Never Amount to Anything* is helping millions of frustrated parents around the globe deal with their challenging child. The key? **Remain positive at all times.**

This week, I dip into Dr. Tim's Mailbag, to share how you can successfully apply my powerful patent-pending positive parenting process to help your own challenging child blossom to almost one quarter of their God-given potential.

Dear Dr. Tim,

I'm a single mother of a challenging 16-year-old named Melanie. Lately, Melanie has morphed from a loving, conscientious student into an impossible-to-manage, moody high school drama queen. I can live with her 11 body piercings—even her 25-inch boa constrictor tattoo that slithers up her thigh. But my former straight-A student's grades have plummeted.

All she does anymore is bitch about me on Facebook. Thanks to her boyfriend named Chainsaw, she now plans to become a circus roadie and insists I call her by her circus name, Viper. What can I do to steer Viper back on track?

Signed, At my wits' end in Wilton

Dear Witless,

I imagine you're rather anxious about your precious Vipemeister's newfound identify and career aspirations to be a carny. But it's important to remain calm and positive. While she may currently despise you as much as I despise Brussels sprouts, before long, she will probably bear Chainsaw's love child and settle down as a mother herself—most likely in some flea-bitten Mexican border town, cohabitating in a circus tent with a 57-year-old alcoholic clown named *Chuckles*, once Chainsaw dumps her for Sword-Swallower Girl.

Then she will have plenty of time to appreciate how great a mom you were and realize in retrospect that you were right about the danger of doing so many drugs. She just needs some time to find herself. Once she is out of prison for dealing, your little angel will come hitchhiking back to the nest. Give her a little time, and by a little time I mean 15 years. As for your concerns about her addiction to Facebook, sadly there is no known cure.

Dear. Dr. Tim,

My nine-year-old boy Travis has serious anger management is-sues. He's been sent to the principal's office seven times in the past four months, most recently for shooting the teacher's pet hamster, Chewbacca, the length of the classroom using his homemade sling-shot. Yesterday, while pitching in a little league game, he deliberately beaned four batters—two of them were on his own team.

He seems obsessed with punching things and shouting about how I'm the worst father in the world because I won't let him watch the Friday the 13th marathon on the Blood 'n Gore channel. How can I help him deal with his anger issues?

Signed, Losing it in Las Vegas

YOU'RE GROUNDED FOR LIFE

Dear Loser,

Wow, I can clearly sense your understandable pride in your son's throwing accuracy. He shows lots of potential to go far as a pitcher. Be sure to encourage that talent. And he constructed that sling-shot all by himself? Sounds like quite the young civil engineer in the making. I would not be too concerned about his temper tantrums. This is very common for boys of his age who possess latent sociopathic tendencies.

As a parent, this sort of behavior might be alarming. But think positively. You just might have a brilliant young electrician in the making – or a mad scientist. Could go either way.

Given his love of animals and a passion for shooting things across large venues, perhaps you should introduce Travis to Viper. I'll bet she can get him a job in the circus getting shot out of a cannon. Stay positive. Frankly, I see nothing wrong with his obsession for slasher movies. He will learn valuable insights about human anatomy and the cardiovascular system. That could come in handy someday in a possible future career as an EMT—or a psychopath.

Dear Dr. Tim,

My six-year-old boy Ernest has taken to flushing things down the toilet. It started innocently enough, flushing marshmallows and such. But lately he's been taking this to alarming levels. Recently he flushed my wife's engagement ring down the toilet, and last week, he flushed my brand new iPod.

I'm starting to get nervous. Nobody has seen Ernest's pet turtle, Bubbles, anywhere since yesterday. Should I be worried?

Signed, Worried in Fort Worth

Dear Ft. Worthless,

First of all, what possessed you to name your son Ernest? No wonder he has issues. But don't worry. Stay calm. Remain positive. Be sure to show support and encouragement for his fascination with plunging things down the toilet. This could be a sign he has a latent interest in a career in plumbing. Plumbers make a very good income—especially the one who charged me for repairs he didn't actually do. Also, I would commend your son on his efforts to give Bubbles his freedom. It's just like that film, *Free Willy*, and I don't mind saying I cried at the end, when Willy was set free. By now, I am sure Bubbles is happily swimming with the fishes.

Well, that's all the time I have today. My wife just brought to my attention that our younger daughter has put our three cats up for sale on eBay, posting, *Buy Buttons and Patches for $100 and we'll throw in Whiskers for free*. She already has a buyer. I must compliment her on her concise marketing ad copy. I see a successful career in advertising in that kid's future. I'm quite positive.

CHAPTER TWO

The Teenage Years—Or "As a Matter of Fact the World Does Revolve Around Me, Dad"

"I solved my low self esteem by becoming arrogant."

Who's the King (or Queen) of Your Castle?

It starts out innocently enough. Your little four-year old princess Tara insists she's scared and can't get to sleep. Can she sleep with mommy and daddy? Pleeeeease? Against your better judgment, you relent and let her snuggle in bed with you—just this once.

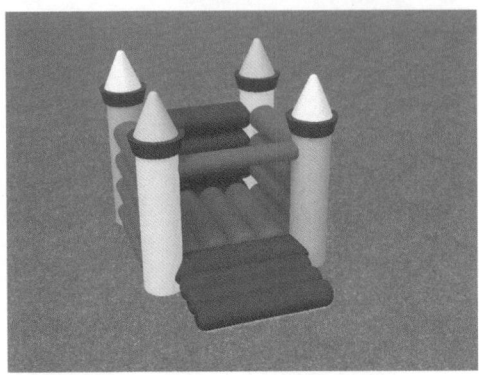

Kevin is seven. This is his castle. For Christmas, he's hoping for a moat filled with alligators – to keep his little sister out. She's so annoying.

Fast forward. Tara, now eight years old, whines about having to eat her peas. Against your better judgment, you let her off the hook and still let her have dessert—after all, it's cookies 'n cream ice cream, her favorite. Before you know it, you wake up one day and your little angel is now a teenager and you suddenly discover that she's running the show, making all sorts of *drop everything* demands that we parents cave into because it's just less work not to engage in another battle. How did this all happen? Personally, I blame it on Obamacare.

I am the father of two high-spirited young girls. I am a highly sought-out parenting expert. My third book, *Timeouts, Tasers and Other Tools of Modern Parenting,* addresses the challenge we face when it seems our teenagers suddenly are in the driver's seat (in some cases literally). Bribery and blackmail are both tactics that I strongly recommend for most confrontations with your teenage offspring. And for you moms (as well as you dads who are in touch with your feminine side), don't underestimate the power of a good display of sobbing. Totally disarms most whiny teenagers. But it takes practice. Start by sniffling and work your way up to the tears.

Take this quiz to determine whether you're still the king or queen of your castle or whether the peasants have stormed the fortress and taken you hostage:

- Do you make special meals for the kids different from what you are having?

- Do you find yourself putting away dishes your kids have left around the house?

- Do you find that your primary role in your kids' lives is to be their personal taxi service, driving them to soccer practice, birthday parties or sleepovers?

- When you want to watch a TV show about the Industrial Revolution, do you immediately change the channel because your 11-year old wants to watch *Gossip Girl*?

- Does your 16-year old leave his towel on the bathroom floor every morning, despite daily reminders to *"HANG UP YOUR TOWEL—I mean it"*?

If you answered **YES** to all of the above, the odds are you are my wife. *(Note to self: Be sure to delete that previous sentence before publishing this article.)* If you answered **NO** to all of the above, this is a strong indicator that you're a pathological liar. Either that or you truly are the *World's Strongest Parent*, in which case, I'm not sure I care to be your friend anymore.

The truth is nowadays, the majority of parents let their kids get away with stuff that would have had most of us packed off to a reform school in years gone by. At some point, most of us parents simply cave, finding it easier to pick up the dirty socks than to nag our kids for the 59th time to do it themselves. Over time, many parents slowly lose the battle for household supremacy. Before we know it, our kids are calling the shots. If this sounds familiar, I'm here to tell you there's hope—not much, I'll grant you, but a glimmer. A tiny, faint, infinitesimal glimmer. Sort of like how Venus looks at night to the naked eye.

Here are just a few of the common mistakes many parents make and what you can do to wrestle back control of your castle from the marauding serfs:

Mistake #2: *Picking up after your teenager when they leave their stuff around the house*

We have all done this one. Your son Jason has taken over the family room with his wrestling team buddies. They scarf down the three major food groups: pepperoni pizza, Mountain Dew and mint chocolate chip ice cream. Movie's over. Friends bolt. Jason heads upstairs, completely oblivious to the smelly socks, sneakers, winter coat, and back pack he left strewn across the room—not to mention pizza crusts, half-empty cans of soda, and a melting carton of ice cream.

You probably scowl. Perhaps you even tell him to come down here this instant and clean up his mess. If you're lucky, you may receive an unintelligible Neanderthalean grunt. Either that or the official two-word response of the modern teenager: *"I know!!!"* But an hour later, *"I know!!"* fades into *"I'll do it tomorrow"* which eventually morphs into *"I forgot."* Next thing you know, you end up cleaning up the mess—because after all, if you don't do it, who will?

Solution: Just pick up anything and everything Jason leaves around the house and deposit it in the giant dumpster known as his bedroom. Within days, the accumulation of dirty socks, stale pizza, flat soda, and food-encrusted dishes should get the message through. And you will watch in amazement as Jason actually starts to clean up his room and put things in the trash. Oh sure he might be so angry with you that he may not talk to you for months—which, if you think about it, could actually be an added bonus. *(Note of caution: In rare instances, this technique may result in permanent bedroom carpet stains, lost silverware, a three-inch layer of dirty clothes on the floor, and a rampant ant infestation.*

YOU'RE GROUNDED FOR LIFE

This technique should not be tried if the offender happens to be this author's younger daughter.)

Mistake #7: *Letting your teenagers leave the dinner table as soon as they have scarfed down their meal in 2 minutes flat, while you're still working on your salad*

When you were young, you ate what your parents served you. And you waited for everyone to finish their meal before leaving the table. When did that tradition fall by the wayside? [Trivia: The correct answer is *May 11, 2003*—although scientists can't quite figure out why.]

Does the following dinner table scene sound familiar? Your 12th grader is checking his phone for messages about the big game, while your 9th grader is texting her BFF about tonight's sleep-over. Before you've finished three bites of chicken, they vanish in a whirl-wind—*"gotta go"*—leaving their half-eaten plates behind for you to rinse and put in the dishwasher.

Solution: Time for some tough love. Implement a new rule: No one leaves the table until both parents have finished. Consider ankle bracelets that attach to the legs of the table. Don't allow any cell phones at the table—unless of course dad needs to check out the score of the Knicks game. Set an example by nicely asking your spouse what happened today. Sure, it may be a bit awkward at first, but eventually you will learn fascinating details about their lives, including *"Today was totally boring"* or *"Anna dumped Carl"* or *I'm pretty sure my Spanish teacher hates me."* Your kids' inquisitive minds will be filled with thought-provoking questions like *"Can I go now?"* and *"How about now?"* and *"How much longer before I can go?"* Yes indeed—quality time around the dinner table. They may grow up resenting you, but at least they'll eat their peas.

Mistake #19: *Helping them with their school project*

Who amongst us does not want to help out our child with their middle school project? Don't tell me that little Tammy Ferguson built her incredible weather station without any help from her dad!

Yeah, right! So there you are, helping your daughter Molly figure out how to paint Saturn. The next thing you know, you're putting the finishing touches on the asteroid belt. Where was Molly all this time? Bragging to Justine on Facebook about how awesome her solar system project is going to be, now that Dad did the whole thing for her. Smooth work, Molly.

Solution: Don't help. Offer lots of encouragement and support. Then go watch the game. Okay, the end result may not be quite as polished. Sure, her solar system has only seven planets. (Seems she missed the part in class that mentioned that Earth was a planet.) So what if the sun orbits around Jupiter? And okay, so in Molly's universe, the asteroid belt is, well, an actual belt.

So what if Molly fails her science project, and as a result fails eighth grade, loses all her self-confidence, bombs her SATs, and can't get into college, as a result of which she ends up homeless and addicted to pain killers. At least Molly didn't cheat on her science project like that Tammy Ferguson did. (I still can't believe Tammy got into Yale. Must be a legacy.)

I'm here to say there *is* hope. We parents need to stand up and remind our teenagers who is paying for the house they live in, the food they eat, and the clothes they are wearing. In other words, we need to do a better job of making our kids feel guilty for everything they have. Show them PowerPoint presentations of starving orphans in Africa. Periodically provide subtle hints that life could be worse, by leaving brochures for reform schools for challenging teens—taped to their bathroom mirror.

So what's **Mistake #1**, you ask? Not telling your kids every single day how much you love them—no matter how much damage they've done to your laptop, your car, or your credit rating. You can never tell them *"I love you"* enough. (But don't forget about those brochures for reform schools. It's sort of a carrot and stick approach.) Most of all, let them know you love them to the ends of the earth, forever and ever—albeit conditionally, depending on whether they made their bed this morning.

Our Summer Vacation—
Only More Interesting

For families everywhere the arrival of September means "welcome back to reality" time. The first week of September usually marks the start of school for most American teenagers, and summer is rapidly vanishing in the rear view mirror. If your summer was like mine, it won't make for an enthralling Holiday letter come December—which is why when it comes to retelling the highlights of your summer, if you weren't able to afford an exotic, envy-inducing adventure, then at least make sure you have an exotic, envy-inducing story about your vacation.

Truth be told, our family's summers are consistently quite lame. Take last summer, for instance. It consisted mainly of listening to our girls whine *"there's nothing to do"* and *"I'm boooooooooooored"*—God knows, life is boring when you live in the scenic Pacific Northwest with all its snowcapped mountains and pristine lakes. Heaven forbid your kids actually go outdoors, ride a bike, swim in the lake or clean their room.

As any loving parent would do, in an effort to insulate ourselves from their constant badgering to "take me to the mall" or otherwise entertain them, we loaded up their summer with leadership / character-building camps and the annual pilgrimage to visit elderly relatives in walkers. That'll teach 'em to whine about being bored.

Any day now, your kids will be returning to school and will confront the inevitable question that every child from a family like mine dreads from friends comparing their summer vacations. I can hear it now:

Sydney: *"Wow, Tim's daughter, what an amazing summer our family had. We went to Africa and slept in a hotel on the side of Mount Kilimanjaro. The room came with a Jacuzzi tub and a Zebra petting zoo. So, what did you do this summer?"*

Tim's daughter: *"I was in summer camp for three weeks as a 'Junior Assistant'. My job was to clean dishes, empty trash, rake leaves, remove rocks, and pull weeds—when I was not cleaning toilets, that is. Ate mostly prison food. Got bitten by mosquitoes so badly that I had to be taken to the hospital (true). Then I visited my grandma in Ohio and played 37 games of Parcheesi with her. She is 97, can't hear and kept thinking the playing pieces were candy."*

Sydney: *"Your summer sounds like a total wipeout. Did I mention our trip to Tahiti in June? I zip-lined through the tree tops of Redwood National Forest and later I parasailed in Acapulco. And when we got home, my parents bought me my own Sea Doo for my 15th birthday."*

My daughter: *"Your own Sea Doo? That sounds way cool. For my birthday, my parents gave me a new pair of work gloves—because the rocks I had to haul at summer camp gave me third degree blisters."*

Sydney: *"Wow, you had the suckiest summer ever. Your parents must be complete losers. I am no longer going to be your friend. Bye now. Hey, Madison, wait up. How was your summer in Fiji? Love your Gucci purse."*

Summers can be traumatizing to your kids when they discover that apparently every other family in their high school except yours took their kids to Disneyworld (the one in France, of course). So, to avoid this trauma of not taking your family on a gloatful (*new word*) Mediterranean cruise to Malta and Santorini, then at least be sure you know how to talk about your more mundane summer vacation in a way that will impress your friends and hopefully keep your teenager from getting re-assigned to the losers' table at lunch—you know—the table you (and when I say **you**, I mean **me**) were assigned to in high school, with members of the "Mathletes" Club.

Say that your big trip was a 1200-mile driving vacation to Darwin, Minnesota to see the world's largest ball of string, then on to Spring Grove, Illinois to snap photos of the world's largest corn maze. Oh sure, in several states, a vacation this dull would be grounds for loss of custodial rights for emotional cruelty to children from the

YOU'RE GROUNDED FOR LIFE

embarrassing taunts they'll be subjected to when they return to school.

You can, however, make up fascinating stories your kids can proudly lie about to their friends. Oh, let's be clear, there is absolutely no way you can tweak the summer's highlights of a big ball of string and a corn maze into anything that sounds remotely like an exciting vacation adventure. Trust me. I already tried. We had to move our kids to another school district as a result of the humiliation they experienced from retelling the story to their school mates. No, the secret is to simply make up a memorable vacation—and make sure your kids don't crack under the pressure of scrutiny when retelling it at school. I've already drafted a rough script. They should have it memorized before school starts:

Let other families take their kids on vacations to Disneyland. Our dream vacation starts with a trip to the World's Largest Pumpkin (since the Largest Wad of Gum museum was closed for repairs).

Sydney: *"So, Tim's daughter, how was your summer? We went to Africa and slept in a hotel on the top of Mount Kilimanjaro. Did I mention our trip to Tahiti in June? Then I did zip-lining through the tree tops of Redwood National Forest, and then I went parasailing in Acapulco. What did you do this summer?"*

My daughter: *"Gosh, Syd. Why so lame a summer? My vacation was a blast, thanks to my loving and financially successful parents. First we went to Cape Canaveral and took a ride in our own private 747, where we simulated weightlessness for two days. That was way cool. Then we went to my parents' private island in the Caribbean owned by Taylor Swift, where we went scuba diving with hump back whales—and Taylor herself. Taylor and I are now totally BFFs. Then we went to the Grand Prix of Monaco, where they let me drive the*

pace car—that was so cool since I don't even have my license yet. I finished fifth, four cars ahead of Danika Patrick.

"Then I went to the FIFA World Cup Soccer Tournament in Brazil where I had box seats right next to Princess Kate Middleton. She is so polite—I had no idea she was a Black Eyed Peas fan. Then when we were in Shanghai, our family got back stage passes to the Lady Gaga concert. Frankly, I thought she was a bit off compared to when we saw her the previous week in Tokyo with Maroon 5.

Oh one more thing. Be prepared to offer your teenage child a small bribe to stick with the scripted vacation story—might I suggest a new go cart or a moped.

Come up with your own incredible story of your summer vacation, and maybe, just maybe, the world will never have to know that your family actually drove the minivan 950 miles to Jackson Township, Ohio to see the world's largest pumpkin. Your secret is safe with me.

YOU'RE GROUNDED FOR LIFE

Dr. Tim, Help Me!
My Daughter Has a Boyfriend....

This week, I dug deep into the Dr. Tim advice column mailbag and came up with the following very informative letter:

Dear Dr. Tim:

My 16-year old daughter now has a boyfriend. Should I kill myself?

Signed,

Terrified in Tacoma.

Thank you for your very detailed and well-constructed letter, Terrified. Can I call you "_Terri?_"

For the rest of you reading this advice column, yes, it's true: along with my expertise in countless other areas, Dr. Tim (it's sort of an honorary title) is also an expert in parenting matters. As the shell-shocked father of not one but two teenage daughters who are both now entering the world of dating, I believe I can shed some insight into Terri's problem. I may even be able to recommend some effective non-hallucinogenic prescriptions for anxiety, depression and anger management that should become a regular part of any parent's daily dietary regimen, starting immediately.

First of all, Terri, I can tell that you did not read my earlier column about the challenge of parenting teenage daughters. Let me share that you're about to embark on some very choppy waters. But there is hope. (_Actually, there is no hope, but if you keep reading this letter, you'll find a coupon for 10% off on my new best seller, Ten Reasons Why You're a Horrible Parent_).

Like most parents of teenagers, you probably hope and pray this day will never come; that your adorable little angels will grow up continuing to idolize you, wanting only to please you and obey your every command until ... oh, say their retirement. Sorry to burst your bubble. Around the age of 12 or 13 (could be sooner or later—your mileage may vary) they start to turn into an alien life form. This is perfectly normal—it simply means that you have completely failed as a parent. Don't worry. Your child is starting to grow up and is preparing to leave the nest. You will then enter the five well-documented stages of Parental Grieving:

Denial >> Anger >> Bargaining > Depression > Giving them your car keys

I have a good friend Ken, who has a daughter named Laura. He told me nostalgically about when Laura first had a crush on a boy. She wore the boy's sweatshirt to bed and doodled his name on her notebook. It sounded so cute. Ken decided to be a responsible dad and look the young man up on Facebook—where he saw photos of the boy's multiple body piercings and a life size nude sculpture he recently did of Brittney Spears, made from 575 crushed beer cans. (I have to give him credit. At least he found a way to recycle his beer cans.) Which brings me to the issue of what boys are after. You might want to sit down, Terri.

News flash: When it comes to dating, teenage boys mainly think about three things: sex, breasts, and ... okay, make that two things. Actually, I conducted some field research into what the average teenage boy (ages 15–19) does in a typical day. The results may surprise you. See the pie chart on the following page.

Surprised? So was I when I made up these statistics. Half of one percent? I had no idea teenage boys spent so much time paying attention to their parents. By the way, there is no truth to the urban legend that the average teenage male thinks about sex every thirty seconds. Research indicates it's way more frequent than that.

So what can you do? Well, you might consider crawling under a large desk and curling up into the fetal position. Let's face it. You're screwed. But before you completely throw in the towel, consider barricading your daughter's bedroom window with titanium alloy-reinforced bars and a security system that goes off when it detects a can of Red Bull or a 12-pack of Trojans within 20 feet.

YOU'RE GROUNDED FOR LIFE

Percent of Time Teenage Boys Spend Each Day In Various Activities
(Ranked Most to Least)

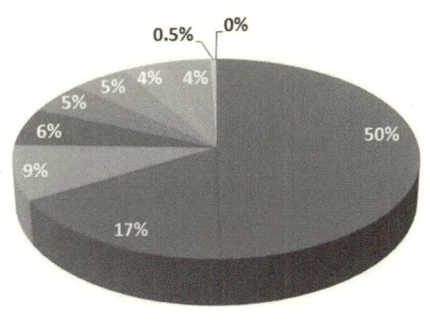

- Think about sex and boobs

- Text or Facebook their friends (mostly about sex and boobs)

- Sleep (includes sleep during class)

- Listen to metal bands "Decaptitated Cockroach Killers" or "Mentally Defective Bunnies" on iPod

- Wolf down junk food not found in nature - with Red Bull Mega-Caffeinated sports drink

- Play sports (including sports games on X-Box)

- Do homework and prepare for tests

- Nag parents to use the car

- Pay attention to what their parents say

- Clean up room and put dirty clothes in laundry

And here are some other practical things you can try:

- Install a 24 x 7 video surveillance system with a GPS tracker ankle bracelet that lets you know any time your daughter has left the boundaries of her permitted visitation destinations—perhaps an ankle tracker with a nice pearl inlay. Style is everything at this age.

- Implement drug testing. Invite the young man to pee into a cup the moment he comes to the door to pick up your precious Charlotte for the homecoming dance. Assuming the stick turns blue, there is nothing for him to worry about.

- Implement a reasonable curfew system—preferably one that requires your daughter to be home roughly an hour before the dance begins.

- Insist that you go along on the date. This one is really effective, and it's a safe bet that this young man won't be asking your angel out again anytime soon. Be sure to offer to pay for the movie and popcorn. It's the least you can do as the dad.

In the end, perhaps the most important thing you can do is teach your daughter the power of the word **NO.** You know—that same word she mastered so well when you asked her to empty the dishwasher, go to bed by 10pm or turn down the volume. Teach her that this very same word can also be used when it comes to boys and sex. Recently Laura had two boys that both wanted to go out with her. One of them is a very nice, polished, well-mannered young man who gets good grades and comes from a very good family and is a member of the high school varsity track team. Let's call him *Harold*. The other young man is, as best as we can tell, the spawn of Satan. When he is not hitting on girls or hitting the bong, he can often be found in juvenile court defending himself against charges typically involving breaking and entering. We'll call him *Demon Seed Boy*.

It has taken my friend Ken countless hours of frank conversations about how Harold really cares about Laura while Demon Seed Boy only wants her as a sexual conquest. But I'm delighted to report that after many patient and loving talks, some firm but compassionate parenting, and the threat that the only car she will be driving until the age of 25 will come with pedals and a bell if he ever catches her so much as giving Demon Seed Boy a furtive glance, Ken thinks his daughter finally has seen the light.

So, Terri, should you give your daughter your blessing to date? Of course not. But what are you going to do? To guide your decision, ask yourself three questions: Is she mature enough to know how to say NO? Does she have the judgment to know good boys from

bad boys? And how long is the waiting list at the *Sisters of the Perpetual Sacred Virgin* convent?

If you have your own parenting dilemma you'd like to share, drop me a note. I am confident I can help you every bit as much as I have helped Terri.

Turn Left NOW! No, Your OTHER Left!!
The Joys of Teaching Your Teenager to Drive.

If you're like me, then you're a 61-year-old male with a receding hairline, with a slight overbite and a two-inch scar on your left hand from a kitchen accident in 2004. But that's beside the point. My point is, if you're like me, then you may also be about to enter one of the most terrifying stages of life: The age when your teenage "child" starts learning how to drive.

Every parent worries about the day their teenager begins to drive. Don't panic. Start by suckering your spouse into agreeing to do this thankless task.

Having somehow endured this traumatic experience with two daughters, I'm happy to say there is a reasonable chance you and your teenager will get through this period un-scathed, and by reasonable chance I mean less than 15%. Let's face it, being a parent is hard enough without having to experience the harrowing adventure of teaching your precious offspring how to drive. But there comes a day when your teenager might utter the phrase every parent dreads: *Hey, Dad. I got into Stanford.* [Ka-Ching!] Even before that day, there is another phrase that terrifies every loving parent: *I want to get my driver's license.*

There is no way to avoid it. Sooner or later, it's going to happen. The sooner you can con, I mean convince, your spouse to sign up for the thankless task of teaching them, the better. In our family, I was the sucker, er, volunteer. As a result of my anguishing experience teaching our daughters how to drive, I've learned several valuable tips to pass on to you.

Tip #1: Don't have children. I can't stress this enough. Oh sure, you may miss out on a few fun things like teaching an impressionable young child how to throw a baseball. But consider the alternative: never having to pay thousands of dollars in car repair bills and jacked-up insurance premiums because there would be no daughter of yours who might be jabbering on her cell phone, thereby accidentally backing your Toyota minivan into your neighbor's mint-condition 1967 Porsche 911 roadster—hypothetically speaking, of course.

Tip #2: Bribe your child. If you did not react in time to apply Tip #1, then do whatever you can to persuade them not to drive until they turn 35. You could make a thoughtful, cogent slide presentation showing the cost-savings of getting a bus pass and the reduced carbon footprint from not driving. Of course, you'll have a greater shot of becoming the next winner of American Idol than convincing your teenager to delay their desire to drive.

So when your slide presentation crashes and burns, proceed directly to Tip #2: bribery. For starters, you might offer to buy them the latest Samsung Galaxy 19G phone if they promise never to drive over 30 mph and only in sunny weather on country roads, with the radio off and no friends in the car. *(This paragraph sponsored by Samsung—makers of the cool new Galaxy 19G.)*

Tip #3: Model safe driving habits. If the first two strategies fail, face it: your kid is going to start driving. So set the standard by modeling proper driving behavior. This means don't crank up the radio full volume or read a map while driving. And never drive 15 mph over the speed limit in a 30 mph zone, failing to come to a complete stop at the stop sign at the intersection of Buford and 27th Place, while talking on your cell phone to your wife about dinner. That driving infraction will cost you a tidy $250. Just trust me on this and please don't ask me any questions.

Tip #4: Remain calm and let 'em drive. There is only so long you can stall by reviewing the location of the warning lights for the 11th time. It's time to let them get behind the wheel. No matter what happens, it is critical for their confidence that you remain calm. So what if your child just barely missed hitting a jogger pushing a baby stroller. Stay calm. Nobody was hurt. So they took that left-hand turn way too tight and almost clipped a police car. Please remain calm.

And so what if they drove a bit too fast as they entered the garage, screeching to a halt only after they ran over... MY BRAND NEW CALLAWAY GOLF CLUBS???!!!??? What the F**k?!!? Don't you tell me to remain calm!! Those were CALLAWAY clubs, for God's sake. I swear the only vehicle she'll be driving for the next century is a Hello Kitty tricycle with training wheels. Ahem, not that my daughter ever did anything like this, mind you.

Tip #5: Help them find a safe car. Young drivers tend to be careless drivers. They make mistakes behind the wheel. So it's important to help them pick out a vehicle that scores well in crash tests and comes loaded with safety features. That's why I strongly recommend purchasing your child a Type 10 MBT Battle Tank, or if you're looking for a bit better gas mileage, perhaps the Alvis FV103 Spartan Armored Personnel Carrier. Choose between two new colors for spring: desert sand and camouflage green. You will sleep soundly knowing your child will never get hurt in a car accident—although I can't rule out the possibility of being taken out by a drone strike.

Good luck as you merge onto the dangerous highway of teenage driving. It can be an anxious time for any parent. That's why I urge you to seriously consider Tip #1. It makes the process so much simpler.

Are All Teenage Daughters Evil?

The adorable girl on the left thinks her daddy is the smartest person in the world. In seven years, she'll turn into the evil person on the right and master the art of eye-rolling and brooding.

Are all teenage daughters evil?

A research study recently reported that people **with teenagers** in the house are, statistically speaking, the **least happy demographic group of all*** It turns out that disgruntled postal workers and prisoners in solitary confinement rank higher in their daily happiness quotient than the average parents of teenagers. Interestingly, Melvin Zemmecki, a disgruntled postal worker currently serving time in solitary at Attica Prison and father of four teenage girls, has the dubious distinction of being rated the most unhappy human being in the USA. *(* Source: My wife told me about this study one morning while I was in the bathroom flossing. My wife would not make up this sort of thing.)*

Not to toot my own horn, but I consider myself an expert in understanding the impact of parenting mistakes and communication failures. As a parent of two teenage daughters, I have the pleasure of witnessing two simultaneous cases of hormonally-induced multiple personality disorder on a daily basis. There are all sorts of theories as to why teenage girls tend to be so moody, angry, irritable, thoughtless, self-absorbed, lazy, disrespectful, emotionally distant, narcissistic, a giant pain in the ass, never EVER cleaning their damn rooms, would it kill you to put your dirty plate in the dishwasher just once, I tell you??!!!??...um, I appear to have forgotten my point.

Oh yes. As I was saying, there are many theories to explain why teenage girls are often challenging and mercurial. Some experts attribute this to the flood of hormones surging through their bodies. Others speculate it's about peer pressure. Some lay the blame at media for promoting an impossible-to-achieve per-fect body image á la Taylor Swift. Some evidence points to the plethora of reality TV shows in which the most selfish, outlandish, nasty, back-stabbing behavior is often glorified and handsomely rewarded.

But I have a different theory: **ALL teenage daughters are evil.**

Okay, okay. Before you jump on your keyboard and pound out an angry rebuttal, let me clarify: What I meant to say is...All teenage daughters are evil—except for my friends, Karen and Jeff's three girls, Marsha, Megan and Morgan—they're angels.

But with that exception, I stand by my theory. Oh sure, my theory, which is only about 27 minutes old, could be colored slightly by the fact that my two daughters had a sleep-over last night with nine of their friends, and our family room looks like the aftermath of Hurricane Katrina. There are enough Doritos, pizza slices, melted ice cream, and half-drunk cans of Diet Pepsi scattered in every nook and cranny of the family room to feed a third world country. Nice job, girls, putting away, *what are the words I'm looking for... oh, right...* **ABSOLUTELY NOTHING!!!**

I have completed an impressive amount of research to support my theory that all teenage daughters at one time or another turn evil. In my case, it seems to have happened around age 13, 7 months and 5 days, when both my daughters changed from the perfect little angels they once were into fashion-obsessed, textaholic teen-agers who spend roughly 87% of their spare time playing games on their iPod or texting other like-minded evil teenagers, leaving approximately 1.5% of their remaining time for being vaguely aware of their parents' existence.

I have conducted exhaustive first-person field research (based mainly on renting the movie *Mean Girls*) to support my thesis that all teenage girls are evil. I actually found that several cities apparently have ordinances requiring girls to turn evil (or at least seriously bitchy) by the time they reach puberty. This ordinance clearly is in effect in Beverly Hills, Orange County, Palm Beach,

Florida, the Hamptons, and oddly enough, Omaha, Nebraska. (I know, that last one surprised me too.)

Now, you may still say, *"Evil"? Really? Isn't that a bit of a stretch?"* Well, I don't mean evil in the *"sociopath stalker kills five, kicks puppy"* sense of the word. No, I mean evil more in the *"You just don't like him because he has a* **purple Mohawk**, *a* **tattoo of a king cobra on his neck** *and a chain that runs from his ear to his nose. You're so judgmental. I hate my life!!"* sort of way.

Here is a quick seven-question test you can administer to determine whether or not your own daughter might currently be evil—and it does not require any urine samples. (Hint—when in doubt, choose "C"; it worked for me on the SATs):

- Has it been more than three months since your daughter last cleaned her room? (Add 10 points if you can no longer determine the type of flooring because you can't actually locate it.)

- Is your daughter thoughtful, considerate and respectful to all non-familial adult authority figures (teachers, coaches, etc.) and is able to maintain this manner effortlessly for hours on end until... precisely the moment she comes through your front door and makes eye contact with you?

- When you gently offer advice for your daughter's agonizing on-again-off-again-on-again-off-again-on-again relationship with [*check the appropriate box:* ___ Chad ___ Jacob ___ Ethan ___ Daniel ___ Blade] is your counsel immediately dismissed out of hand with the phrases *"Forget it, Dad. You just don't get it!!"* [Insert the mandatory accompanying eye roll here.]

- Has she told you more than once in the past 24 hours how ***borrrrrr-ing*** school is, that she doesn't see the point to going anymore, and is considering catching a bus and moving to Florida with snake-tattoo boy beau [*check the appropriate box:* ___Chad ___ Jacob ___ Ethan ___ Daniel ___ Blade] because *"I can take care of myself."*

- Have you wondered quietly to yourself more than twice in the past week, *"Who is this girl in my kitchen wolfing down stale potato chips and Mountain Dew for breakfast, and what have they done with my daughter?"*

- When you enter her room to say goodnight, tell her you love her, and kiss her on the top of her head, does she lovingly respond by shrieking *"Geez, you're ruining my hairdo! Go away! And close the door behind you!"*

- Do you routinely find yourself shouting: *"**You're NOT leaving this house wearing that!!**"* as your daughter attempts to sneak out wearing a miniskirt that does not quite reach three inches below her navel?

If you answered YES to six or more of these questions, your teenage daughter currently is, statistically speaking, evil. (For full disclosure, this test has a statistical margin of error of +/- 97%).

But don't worry—if your daughter scored **EVIL** or just **Moderately Wicked,** most of the time this turns out to be a phase they outgrow as soon as they have evil daughters of their own or five years after your death, whichever comes last.

So, are most teenage girls truly evil? Perhaps not. Perhaps my judgment is clouded by the latest Category 4 hormonal hurricane that just blew through my living room this afternoon screaming *"You never do ANYTHING for me"* in response to my calmly worded observation, *"No, I will not buy you an iPad Mini just for making your bed."*

Although I might not be able to compete with the boy with the dragon tattoo for my daughters' attention anymore, there are those rare moments of hope. Like when I drive my teen daughter to soccer and she gives me a kiss, saying, *"I love you, Daddy."* Just then—at that precise moment, maybe, just maybe, she's not completely evil after all. And maybe I'm not the worst parent in the world. That award would go to my brother-in-law, Eddie.

Meet the World's Smartest Person: My Teenage Daughter

Personally, I can't stand it when other people brag about their kids. You'll never catch me puffing up my chest about my daughter winning the National Chess Tournament for kids seven and under. Nor will you ever hear me boast about her eighth grade science experiment, inventing an internal combustion engine that ran on tap water. You'll never hear me talk your ear off about my daughter scoring four goals to lead her team to victory in the state soccer championships either. That's because I hate to brag about my kids' incredible achievements (particularly when it involves making it all up).

But the one thing I have to admit to taking pride in is the fact that I am—much to my surprise—the parent of the world's smartest person. I'm talking about my teenage daughter Rachel. I base this conclusion on more than a decade of longitudinal field studies observing her interaction with my wife and me. At first, I was not fully aware of just how superior her intellect was—in part because at the age of four, she still believed in unicorns and was convinced we should trade in her younger sister for an Easy Bake oven.

Over time, however, it became clear just how amazingly bright she was compared to her stupid parents—because she made a point of reminding us of that fact on a daily basis. For years, I lived under the misconception that earth revolved around the sun. But by the time Rachel hit her teens, it had become obvious to me—the entire universe revolved around *her*.

It was actually not until Rachel turned 13 that her claim to being the smartest person in our house was made official (by Rachel). She told me one day that she realized she had been wrong about something she'd said two years earlier. She modestly admitted, "Oh yeah, that was a couple years ago, back before I knew every-thing." (A direct quote.)

Looking back, the evidence of her superior intellect was all around me. When Rachel was six, I would often suggest that she share her toys with her younger sister. However, she was convinced this was a stupid idea, because her research concluded that her younger sister Emmy was a monkey-brained, poopy-headed worm monster who would break all her toys. Then, one day, while Rachel was pulling on Emmy's hair and eating all of her sister's candy, Emmy took Rachel's Barbie doll and bit its head off. Rachel used this opportunity to point out the absurdity of her father's misguided premise of the value of sharing one's toys.

When Rachel turned eight, she successfully proved her hypothesis that if you whine, beg, badger, gripe, complain, pester, and whimper endlessly for four months, your parents will eventually break down and get you a kitty—and let you name it Rainbow Cutie because that's the best kitty cat name in the world.

When she was 10, she invented an ingenious contraption she named the *Boy Catcher* (designed to ensnare any unsuspecting boy who foolishly set foot in her room), using nothing more than paperclips and string. (True!) Sadly she was never able to patent her brilliant invention.

Here is my little genius girl Rachel getting ready for take-off, with Emmy cheering her on. Alas, not quite enough sparkle dust on her wings to reach outer space. Keep trying.

By age 12, her artistic brilliance shined brightly in the form of an amazing piece of abstract artwork she created on a canvass consisting of her bedroom floor. She used a most unusual combination of common household items, including 27 dirty socks, three dozen crayons, a half-eaten box of Cheez-its, an unopened yogurt container that had expired five years prior, a Valentine card

from some boy named Kenny from second grade who apparently eluded her Boy Catcher, sixteen dollars and twenty seven cents in dimes, nickels and pennies, a diary opened to a page with the heading *"Why my parents are the worst parents in the world,"* and every t-shirt she had ever worn since first grade.

When Rachel turned 15, I errantly suggested to her that the best way to succeed and be happy in life might be to study hard, get good grades and get into a good college. Of course, I was wrong. The best way to be happy, according to my daughter, was to stay up until 3:30am on a school night posting on Facebook, drinking three cans of Red Bull, and texting her girlfriends about what a bitch Samantha was for not inviting her to the party.

By age 17, she argued with impressive conviction about how antiquated my views were about dating and sex. I had always thought that the best boys were the ones with good grades, good manners and at least periodically maintained personal hygiene. But Rachel knew that the best boys were the ones with multiple body piercings and tri-color hair who had been kicked off the football team.

Ever since she was old enough to know how to record *Sponge Bob Square Pants* over the *West Wing* episode I had been waiting all week to watch, my daughter has constantly pointed out to me that she was way smarter than her dad—not to mention that every piece of parental advice I'd ever offered was totally lame. I had no idea she had garnered infinite wisdom about life and love by the age of 13. After years of constantly reminding me that she had all the answers, I finally accepted that she must indeed KNOW EVERYTHING! So, pardon me if I boast about being the proud papa of the world's smartest person.

But I have to say, I'm starting to worry just a little bit. I visited my daughter last month at college, where she is now a senior, and on three separate occasions I offered up a suggestion...with which she totally agreed. Uh-oh. Perhaps my perfect little genius is not quite as brilliant as she used to be. Or perhaps I am just getting smarter.

CHAPTER THREE

Off to College—Or "Dear Dean of Students, Please Keep My Child"

"Your son, running screaming from the real world, is home."

Four Strategies for Saving for Your Kids' College Education

About 21 years ago, my wife and I committed a horrible lapse of financial judgment. We are still paying for this reckless mistake these many years later: We became parents. At first it seemed like a great idea—staring into the innocent, helpless eyes of our two adorable angel babies adopted from China.

This hat costs approximately $80,000. Buy a Red Sox baseball cap instead and save $79,985. If you ask me, a much better value.

If only someone had intervened—stopped me from boarding that plane for Hong Kong—and pointed out that over the next 21 years, these little cherubs would morph into retirement-savings-draining, eye-rolling, "take me to the mall now" moody, fashion-obsessed drama queens who could legally drive my car while illegally texting their friends about how lame their parents were...if only somebody had intervened back then and told me what we would be in for, I would have undoubtedly made...the same reckless decision. But that's beside the point.

My point is this: Raising kids is expensive. The return on your college investment is highly speculative at best, particularly when you learn your son is majoring in Medieval French Gender Studies. For many parents a far less risky investment would be betting their entire life savings on the trifecta in the second race at Belmont Park.

Back in the seventies, when I went to college, the cost of a year's tuition—even for an out-of-stater like me—was comparable to the cost of a nice drum set. Now, to send a child to an out-of-state university or a private college costs roughly the same as the GDP

YOU'RE GROUNDED FOR LIFE

of say, New Zealand. *[Author's Correction: I apologize. The previous statement was a gross exaggeration. I meant to say **the North Island** of New Zealand.]*

The cost of a college education is rising at a meteoric pace. By some conservative estimates, it is escalating by approximately **26% each month.** (And by "conservative estimates" I mean estimates I just made up as I was typing the previous sentence.)

If you were smart enough not to make my disastrous financial mistake by choosing never to have kids in the first place, kudos to you. It must be nice to imagine retiring before age 75 with more than just your stamp collection for savings. Feel no guilt whatsoever about buying that 28' power boat—with cash—while I try to figure out whether our family can afford the extravagance of Pizza Hut this evening, given that we just went to the Olive Garden last month.

But if you made that all-too-common costly mistake of deciding to raise a family, and you have kids nearing college age, many of the following questions may sound familiar:

- How will we save enough to provide our kids with a good college education?

- If we can only send one of our three kids to college, which one do we love most?

- Why did I listen to my wife when she insisted we sell all our Microsoft stock back in 1989?

- How can our neighbor afford to send two kids to Ivy League schools on a teacher's salary? Are they dealing drugs? Should I notify the police?

- Why did I ever go to that time share presentation in Vegas? That's $10,000 I'll never get back.

- What is the state capitol of West Virginia?

Do these questions sound familiar? (By the way, it's Charleston. I know that was bothering you, too.) To save you countless years of anxiety over how you will save up enough money to pay for your kids' college educations, I wanted to share four time-tested strategies you won't hear from that hack personal investment huckster Suze Orman:

Strategy 1: Acquire one million dollars. Admittedly, this strategy may be more of a challenge for some of you than others. If you happen to have made a fortune by inventing Skype or perhaps you know a millionaire you are comfortable blackmailing, this would be an ideal place to begin. This should be enough to cover at least the first two years of college, with enough left over for a few nice dinners out at Outback Steakhouse when you come to visit.

If you are a stay at-home parent, and your spouse's income is not nearly enough to cover the cost of college—say your hubby writes a humor blog—consider divorcing your spouse for an older, wealthier mate. I might suggest an oil executive, just about any hedge fund manager from Goldman Sachs, or perhaps a graying, former Hollywood A-lister like, say, Kevin Costner. While at first this may hurt your spouse's feelings, as soon as they realize they no longer have to cover the college bills, they'll wonder why you waited so long to divorce them. Besides, Kevin Costner is actually quite a decent fellow, from what I've read in People Magazine.

Strategy 2: Cut back on non-essential spending. Look for areas of discretionary spending that you can put on hold. Does your spouse really need to have that heart bypass operation next week? Here are a few other tried 'n true ideas: Skip dinners in months ending in the letters "r" or "y". Cut back on your water consumption by only showering in summer months. At Christmas, save money on expensive gifts by handcrafting personalized presents from common household items. (But be careful. I tried this last year—gave my girls friendship bracelets made of pipe cleaners and colored string. They would not speak to me for two weeks.)

Strategy 3: Re-define "a quality education." Convince your kids that all the elite colleges contain the word "Community" in their name. This simple technique could save you more than $50,000 in the long run.

Remind them repeatedly not to be duped by the insidious propaganda of marginal institutions like Yale, Princeton, Columbia, Brown, and Dartmouth. Those schools all suck. They just have slick marketing departments. The fact they all rejected me is beside the point. Trust me, they all totally suck. Suck, suck, suck. Look at their football programs if you don't believe me.

Strategy 4: Consider rewarding alternatives to a college education. Praise your kids as often as possible for their emerging non-academic talents. Comment casually how gifted a pizza delivery driver you think they could be someday if they played their cards right. Leave pamphlets describing pet-sitting as a career. Tell them how you can envision them becoming a superstar coffee drive-thru barista. Don't forget to mention all the tip money they can earn.

The sky's the limit (so long as the job doesn't require a diploma). Remind them of how much more exciting it would be to become an assistant cashier at Build-A-Bear than having to sit through dull, boring college classes like accounting, mechanical engineering or the sociology of Renaissance festivals.

If you simply can't amass the savings to afford paying for college, I might suggest getting your child to focus on stimulating activities other than their studies—perhaps mastering *World of Warcraft XII* or watching the first ten seasons of *Grey's Anatomy* instead of studying for finals. You may just discover that all your worries about paying for a college education have miraculously vanished into thin air. Good luck!

My Failsafe Five-Step Strategy to Guarantee Your Kid a Spot in Princeton

Don't let your kid's 2.97 GPA deter you. Your senior can still get into an Ivy League School with this five-step plan. Step 1: Make sure he's the grandson of the university's President.

Every fall, when school is back in session, high school seniors are scrambling to pull together college applications. It's an anxious time for parents like me. Some parents may be sweating more than others. Take my over-achieving Microsoft senior executive next door neighbors, The Wongs (recent immigrants from Shanghai). They're frantically hoping their little violinist, chess champion daughter Li gets into Harvard or Yale.

Even with her staggering 6.8 GPA (I have no idea how either), in this competitive environment, Li might have to settle for her safety school, Oxford. In our family's case, we were just hoping we didn't have to fall back on our daughter's safety school, the Louisiana Truck Driving & Secretarial Academy.

Our expert staff of college planning advisors and part-time Wal-Mart greeters has assembled a strategy _guaranteed_ to get your child into the **Ivy* League** college of their choice _(* we're talking of course about **Ivy** Tech Community College with 30 campuses throughout Indiana)._

First, a word about your student's 2.75 GPA: Chill. Let's face it, by now three-fourths of your high school senior's cumulative GPA is behind them. Sure, they probably should have taken _Advanced Placement Anatomy & Physiology_ last semester instead of _Intro to Pickleball_, but how could they have known at age 17 that _Anatomy & Physiology_ might come in handy down the road...in their career plans...to become an anatomical physiologist?

YOU'RE GROUNDED FOR LIFE

So let's help your super star get into the college of their parent's dreams. (Let's worry another day about the fact they'll probably flunk out after second semester.)

Strategy #1: The SAT Test: When in Doubt, Choose A, B, C or D. A student's standardized test score is one of the most important factors colleges consider when deciding to reject my daughter's application. When taking this test, I strongly advise your future Einstein limit their response options to one of the first four letters of the alphabet. [Hint: "**Q**" is almost never the right answer.] You might also want to have them sit right next to junior chess champion Li Wong. She scored a 2370 on her PSAT. Capiche?

Strategy #2: The College Essay: Recently colleges have been placing increasing importance on the college essay—in order to get an idea of what your child is *passionate* about. I'm not sure your wunderkind Dustin is setting the world on fire with his *passion* for playing Halo2 on his Xbox 360 with his best friend Lucas until 2am. Your student's college essay must show true passion and must include at least one of the following story elements:

- How their near brush with death during their solo climb to the summit of K-2 at age 14 to raise money for starving kids in New Jersey helped them become aware of the imminent threat of global warming

- How their concern for the third world cultures grew out of their experience of building a church (or, if you prefer, synagogue) at age 16 for a lost Amazonian tribe, using only a nail file, duct tape, and a tube of crazy glue

- How at age 15 they saved a pod of orca whales from certain death at the hands of a team of Halliburton black ops, teaching her the importance of saving the planet, one Halliburton mercenary at a time

- How at age 11 they delivered food to thousands of homeless families via a drone they'd constructed from paper clips and tin foil

Strategy #3: Letters of Recommendation: I used to be mildly concerned when every teacher said the same thing about our child: *"No, I can't say that I recall ever having her as a student."* Until I realized that the secret is to compose these letters of recommendation myself. Who knew your child was such a super star? Read these achievements we just made up about your precious angel. Are you blushing yet?

- "As [name of child]'s soccer coach for the past 11 seasons, I have never seen a more gifted athlete, natural born leader or humanitarian left striker. Despite playing with a broken femur for most of last year, I doubt her record of 57 goals in a season will ever be broken...."

- "I consider myself blessed to have been [name of child]'s Bio-Chem-Physics-Modern Dance teacher. Not only was he / she a joy to have in class, but he / she is my first student ever to have discovered a new chemical element. But it was her dissertation disproving Einstein's theory of relativity that impressed me the most...."

- "As Governor of the fine state of [insert state name], I can't say enough positive things about [name of child]. If you accept his / her application, I believe I just might be able to locate an additional $1.5 million in grant money in the budget earmarked for your university. Let's keep this just between you and me, okay...." When fabricating a letter from an important official, pick one who's been shamed out of office. Less likely they can be tracked down.

Strategy #4: Volunteerism / Community Service: Hopefully by now, you're catching on. Not sure your daughter's selfless gesture "volunteering" to drive her friends to the mall is quite what they mean by volunteerism. Try one of these creative ideas in your child's application instead:

- I spent the summer in Mexico [or Gulf Coast or Newark, NJ] building homes for people displaced by Hurricane [*Insert name here*]. Choose a credible-sounding name. Good

choices: *Hurricane Isaac, Charles, Amanda*. Poor choices: *Hurricane Buddy, Tootsie, Voldemort*.

- I interned at the zoo, nursing back to health [choose between: baby penguins / baby pandas / baby tiger cubs] that had been badly injured in [choose between: a torrential flood / a devastating monsoon / a Mexican circus animal juggling act gone horribly awry].

- I worked last summer at a refugee camp in Kenya where I made hand-woven baskets for disadvantaged Kenyan orphans, who used the baskets to rescue baby animals injured in circus animal juggling accidents.

Strategy #5: Unique Characteristics that Set Your Child Apart: Ask yourself: What sets your child apart—besides the fact he / she was the first student ever to fail *Intro to Pickleball*? Get creative. Here are some of our personal favorites:

- Your child's a multi-racial orphan you adopted at age 9 from a downtrodden West African nation (I might suggest Senegal—it's very trendy right now with Admissions Officers.) For a nice finishing touch, scan a photo of a smiling African teenager from any recent National Geographic magazine.

- At age 14, they overcame a debilitating childhood stutter and now perform Shakespeare in the Park on weekends for elderly shut-ins.

- At age 13, they wrote the source code for Google's search engine algorithm, before becoming Facebook's youngest programmer. The Thumbs up LIKE button was their idea.

Follow this five-step strategy, and your kid is a shoe-in for Princeton. As to how you'll ever scrape up the $50,000 a year to pay for it, I'll get back to you on that.

College Essentials Packing Checklist…. Item 756: Their Fourth Grade Seashell Collection

Every year around late August, thousands of families endure an emotionally trying ritual: Sending their high school graduate off to college—or in the case of my neighbor Bert Zablinski's under-achieving boy Freddie, a four-week correspondence course for road construction flag operators. For many distraught parents it means driving hundreds of miles in a tightly cramped car filled with college gear, then coming to a startling realization they forgot to bring one essential item: Their child. Don't let this happen to you.

The experience of sending your offspring to college is different for every family. But there is one feeling almost every parent shares: a desperate hope they'll have the winning Powerball lottery tickets so they can pay for college. That's their Plan A. Most parents don't have a Plan B, now that the average cost of four years of college recently surpassed the GNP of Uruguay.

Last week, my wife Michele (who hates when I mention her by name when I write, so will hereafter be referred to as Jasmine) and I joined these ranks. We sent our eldest daughter off to **Washington State University** (which hates when I mention their institution by name in this column, so will hereafter be referred to as Princeton). We drove our child 650 miles to her dorm at WSU, er, Princeton (actually it's only 300 miles—we missed a few exits) and helped her move in. Before I knew it, I was back home, staring sadly at her empty bedroom, facing a bleak new reality: Now I would be the one who has to scoop the kitty litter, empty the dishwasher and take out the trash. God, I'll miss her.

When your turn comes to ship your child off to college, learn from my experience. Consider FedExing your student. Be sure to use plenty of bubble wrap. Here are a few more helpful tips:

YOU'RE GROUNDED FOR LIFE

Create a packing checklist.

You'd be amazed at how many things your child will need when they head off to college. If your child is a girl, consider the following essentials: a hair dryer, curling iron, some other device that looks exactly like a curling iron but she'll tell you is a hair straightener, a second hair dryer, in case the first one accidentally gets left at the McDonald's in Nowheresville, USA en route to her dorm.

Be sure to pack enough variety of clothing to last your child through at least six presidential elections because apparently there are no washing machines within a 500-mile radius **When packing for college, remind your child to take only what they absolutely need, like 25 pairs of shoes, three boxes of stuffed animals, and a ping pong table.**

of her dorm. Other essentials include a five-year supply of Top Ramen and Cup O' Noodles, along with every last roll of toilet paper she was able to sneak out of our house.

Might as well let her pack that drum set you bought her in 8th grade, which she only used twice. You never know when she might decide to switch her major from international business to African Tribal Annoying Banging Sounds. One thing that for sure will NOT be on your child's packing list: a photo of mom and dad. You might want to sneak that into one of her nine purses, to remind her you once existed.

Bring a hand truck for the move-in.

Since you needed a U-Haul truck the size of an armored personnel carrier to fit all your child's crap, you'll need something to haul it all to her dorm room. While these days college dorms have Wi-Fi internet, they don't have elevators. We were delighted to learn upon arrival that our daughter's room was on the 11th floor. So for us, the hand truck was indispensable—for the entire eleven minutes it remained in our possession—until other families concluded it must have been *Property of Princeton University* and started using it the moment I turned my back to unpack the fifth box of shoes.

Reserve some private time for a parental chat.

This may be the last time you see your child for many months (unless you're Freddie Zablinski's parent). They're about to set off on an exciting adventure. Use this last opportunity to share precious insights to guide them to make good choices on life's road ahead. Let me suggest some possible mentoring topics:

- Be tolerant of people with different world views from yours. You will meet all sorts of people here.

- Study hard, get good grades, but make sure you maintain a balance. Don't burn yourself out.

- Have fun. And by fun, I mean wholesome fun, like backgammon, not tequila shots in a wet T-shirt contest at the *I Phelta Thigh* frat house.

- If I ever find out you've been doing drugs of any kind, kiss goodbye to our paying for college, missy.

- Hey, what the hell? Are those *my* TaylorMade golf clubs? I want them back—*now!*

Don't stay too long.

As emotional as this experience will be, resist the temptation to overstay your welcome. Your child is anxious to begin her new life, meet new friends and start telling them stories about how annoying her parents are. Once you've finished lugging the last crate of Diet Coke up to their 11th floor dorm room, take some time to enjoy your child's company—and by "take some time" I mean four

minutes. Any longer and you're starting to crowd her newfound independence. Then get back in your car—it will be easy to locate. It'll be the one with the bright red $75 parking ticket for exceeding your 60-minute unloading time limit by two minutes.

For many parents like Miche- er, Jasmine and me, the trip home can be the hardest part—knowing that your little angel is all grown up, reflecting on how the years raced by far too quickly and how she never did return your golf clubs. But don't get too choked up. I understand your little princess is going to a community college—nine miles from home. She'll be back next Saturday to ask you to do her laundry and to borrow your credit card for a few more essential items. So try to hold it together for the next seven days, won't you?

Preparing for Life as an Empty Nester (and Hoping for an Occasional Text from My Kids)

Our girls are all grown up and off to college. My job as parent is officially over. I won't have to worry about them ever again... yeah, right!

This weekend I have the whole house to myself. Our kids are both in college and my wife is away. For the past few days, it's been eerily quiet—and eerily tidy. It's weird to walk into the bathroom and not see my daughter's curling iron, wet towels and jars of makeup piled up in my sink. I barely recognize the kitchen now because there are no stacks of dirty dishes covering every square inch of the counter.

For the first time in 19 years, there are no kids in our house. We've joined the ranks of a rapidly growing demographic: Happy People (otherwise known as "Empty Nesters"). Many couples look forward to this phase of life. But for me, it's been a difficult adjustment.

So I took time this weekend to look at photo albums and watch family videos. It brought back wonderful memories of many cherished times with our daughters.

Like the 1,284 diaper changes (which, according to my rough estimate, is approximately 1,284 more times than my father changed his own kids' diapers).

Or, speaking of diapers, the time I was lying on the bed holding our baby Emily over my head, staring into her eyes as she beamed an innocent smile, right before she had a volcanic eruption of poop. Now, of course, that would not have been a problem had she

been wearing diapers under her pajamas. Unfortunately, however, someone (my wife Michele's name is being withheld to protect her identity) accidentally neglected to put diapers on her. Someday, perhaps years from now, when I have forgiven my wife, I no doubt will laugh about this.

Or the time Rachel, then three, decided to help her daddy water the house plants by hauling our garden hose indoors, then proceeding to water the plants...and the living room carpet...and the wood floors...and her sister's diaper...and the TV...and the cat.

Or the time Emily, age five, decided she wanted to give herself a new look and cut off all the hair on the left side of her head. We had to shave off the other half so that people wouldn't think she was being raised by drug-addled Goth punkers. Then strangers complimented us on our cute son.

Or the time Rachel, age eight, was learning to throw a baseball and decided that the perfect time to play catch with daddy was while he had his back to her, shaving in the bathroom. Her wild pitch ended up shattering our bathroom mirror. But I have to say, I was impressed by her form. Pretty sure it was a split finger curve ball.

Or the time when Emily was nine that I taught her to ride a bicycle. Every dad treasures this moment. I remember proudly watching my little girl as I shoved her off and yelled, *"Keep pedaling. You're doing great!!!"* just before she veered sharply right, screaming in terror, and smashed into our neighbor's tree. She barely needed seven stitches, but the experience somehow traumatized her about getting back on a bike for several years. Even more tragically, the tree is still in therapy.

Or the time I took Rachel golfing for the very first time on a real golf course. I remember it so well. We went to the driving range to warm up. She reached for her driver, which was stuck in her golf bag. When she finally pried it out, the club head slammed into her forehead, resulting in a severe concussion. We never did make it to the first tee, but the accident spared her from the even deeper emotional scars of actually playing golf (which I know only too well). So it all worked out.

Or the many times over the past ten years I counseled Emily about ways to organize her bedroom more efficiently. Her room at the best of times resembled a village after a tsunami. We would often engage in delightful banter as she would "evaluate" *[translation: "ignore"]* my suggestions about ways to remove articles of dirty clothing and three-week old pasta to make it possible to actually see the dirt on the carpet; and then I would cheerily remind her who paid for this house and inquire how she planned to pay for college on her own.

Or the proud day when Rachel, age 16, earned her learner's permit, and we celebrated by having her drive me home from the DMV test center. It was a lovely summer day. I remember it so well, especially the somewhat abrupt ending to our drive, when Rachel smashed the car into a landscaping rock as she pulled into our driveway. That was $1,400 in repairs that I will never forget. Ah, precious memories.

I miss my daughters, now that it's just Michele and me alone in the house. Our lives just aren't the same without their laughter, smiles, and text messages at 12:15am on a Saturday night saying *"I need a ride home from Alice's house NOW!"*

I can't believe that my little girls are leading their lives on their own and will no longer be under our roof—or on top of our roof, as we scream and wave at them not to move until the fire department arrives with a ladder.

I am doing my best to adjust to my quieter life. I just might have to call my kids now and then, perhaps from the deck of a cruise ship somewhere in the Mediterranean...with my own private bathroom and with not a single piece of my daughter's dirty underwear in the sink.

My wife and I miss them dearly. But we'll just have to manage on our own...to pay for their college tuition, housing, car insurance, and cell phone bills.

A Parent's Survival Guide for When Your College Kid Comes Home for the Holidays

Recently both of our daughters came home for the holiday break. Their return brought us a new set of parenting concerns. When kids go off to college, they suddenly consider themselves adults. They feel the old *kids' rules* from their high school years no longer apply. So it can be stressful to know how to parent your almost-adult child now that they've concluded they no longer need to listen to a word you say. That's why, in the most loving way possible, you should periodically remind them—roughly every two hours—about who is paying for their college and how you'd be delighted to spend that money on a Mediterranean cruise for yourself if they don't clean up their act during their brief time home.

Look at this friendly college student helping out his parents by doing the dishes. Okay, technically he's a paid actor. I couldn't find an actual photo of a college kid helping with chores.

I would like to share my best parenting advice for how to get your kids to cooperate when they come home from college. I really would. But I can no more decipher the code for how to parent college-age kids than I can explain why some people pay $200 more for a cell phone custom-colorized to match their purse. But I will try to impart some wisdom just the same.

Challenge #1: The pit stop. Many parents experience the short-lived joy of welcoming their kids home for winter break only to become annoyed as their child vanishes seconds after their arrival, shouting, *"Hi, Dad. Gotta go. Meeting Bridget at the mall."* It's easy to feel like your kids are only using your house as a place to crash at night, but that's not true. They are also using your house for the free food, free laundry service, and free use of your Lexus. Oh, and just in case you were wondering whether your child might be heading off to shop for a Christmas present for you—they're not. They're going to Victoria Secret for some new thong underwear. Trust me. You don't want to know the details.

The key is to be patient. Your child is growing up, by which I mean they are turning into a narcissistic young wise ass who thinks the world owes them a college education, and they can come and go as they please with no responsibilities. So you just gave them $100 spending money, along with the keys to your Lexus simply because they begged you *"pretty please, Daddy"*—you're still not getting a present. Let it go.

Challenge #2: The messy bedroom. Another frustration many parents share (and by "many parents" I mean this writer) is how when their kids come home from college, they have somehow forgotten all the rules about keeping their room clean. Within 24 hours of arriving home, their room suddenly looks like a crime scene in which every square inch has been ransacked in a desperate search to locate the missing Hope Diamond.

You ask them to clean up and they say something like, *"I know. Chillax, dude. I'll do it when I get back from Trevor's party"* which, when translated using the Google Teenager-to-Parent language translator, means "over my dead body." Once again, be patient. Your son is still figuring out this thing called adulthood. And no, I have no idea how he sneaked that beer keg into his bedroom closet. But I'm confident he'll dispose of it just as soon as he and his five buddies—who somehow ended up crashing on your living room floor last night—have consumed the rest of the beer—which should be shortly before noon.

Challenge #3: The boyfriend/girlfriend. Now that your precious little angel has morphed into a self-righteous college student who is way smarter than their parents, it's understandable that they

might think they have achieved the status of adulthood and all the privileges that come with it, including having their boyfriend/girlfriend sleep in their bedroom under your roof.

This confusion is understandable because despite the 27 times you've said *"under no circumstances is a boy EVER allowed to sleep in your room unless that boy is your husband and the year is 2025"*, she never quite understood that this provision was meant to remain in effect beyond age 18. And she's now 18 and four months—and legally allowed to vote. So she votes that Blake can stay overnight in her bedroom. See? It's just a simple misunderstanding—one that can quickly be ironed out by means of a long, heated shouting match involving cogent debate points about how you're the worst parent in the world and a murderer of love. Good luck getting that Christmas gift now, dad.

Challenge #4: The chores negotiation. When they were younger, you told your kids you needed them to help with the chores, and they dutifully complied. Remember? Okay, perhaps I'm confusing your family with an episode of *The Waltons*. Now that your child is back home for Christmas break, don't count on them to help with the vacuuming... or making dinners...or spending one second with the family on Christmas day past the clock strike of noon (after they have slept until 11:30am).

Now that they're in college and can legally drink hard alcohol (if they moved to Lithuania), they consider themselves fully emancipated. And every request turns into a negotiation—including your request that they try to act nicely to their younger sibling, for which they will most likely demand an exorbitant fee.

It's normal that they will push back when you ask for their help doing the dishes or, say, feigning consideration for anybody else's needs while they are visiting. That's because, let's face it, there's just not enough time for them to see all their friends, crash four rave parties, watch every episode of *Game of Thrones*, and still find time to help out around the house. Something's got to give—like helping anyone related to them.

But you are still the parent. There are times when you simply need to lay down the law and remind your child that there is no such thing as a free lunch—ignoring the irony that during their entire visit, *every* lunch has in fact been free. Let them know gently but firmly that they will need to help out around the house if they expect you to keep paying for college. If you're firm, they'll respect you. No, just kidding. They won't. But you just might get them to take out the trash once before they head back to college. Personally, I'd settle for them remembering to get rid of the beer keg in their bedroom closet. It's starting to smell gross.

Lessons in Bonding

Recently my college-age daughter Rachel emailed me, asking for help with a problem. Such an event—being rarer than a sighting of Halley's Comet—calls for all-hands-on-deck-full-throttle parental engagement. "I'm there for you, Rachel."

Thus began an email exchange that I am proud to say profoundly impacted my daughter and our relationship. Her gratitude for my sage advice is evidenced in her words that, well, she couldn't even put into words how helpful I was.

Rachel: Hey, Dad. Wanted to ask you something. My boyfriend Brad and me had a fight. I saw him with my best friend Brianna. They were holding hands. He says she's just a friend, but I think he's lying. Should I confront him?

Me: Thanks for your email, Rachel. I am happy to help. Frankly, this is a common problem for many young people. In fact, your mom often struggled with similar issues when she was your age.

Here are my suggestions. First, never start a sentence with a verb unless it's a command. When you write *"Wanted to ask you something"*, the reader is left wondering: *Who* wanted to ask me something? My daughter? My boss? A strange man in a tall hat? You never want to leave your reader guessing.

Also it's not *"Brad and **me** had a fight."* It's "Brad and **I**." Me is the objective form of the first person pronoun. In this context, however, you need the subjective form.

Rachel: Whatever, Dad. I don't think you understand. I think Brad is cheating on me. Last nite, I texted him. No reply. No idea what he's up 2. What should I do?

Me: Well, I can think of a couple things to do. First, consider using Spellchecker. It would have caught your misspelling of *"night"* immediately. Secondly, you have a dangling preposition in that same sentence, which you compounded by writing the number "2" when you meant the word *"to."* Try rephrasing your sentence this way: *"I have no idea what Brad is doing."*

Rachel: I don't care about dangled propositions, Dad. I want you to really listen to me. Do you understand my problem?

Me: Yes, I think I do. Your problem is that you have a split infinitive in your sentence *"I want you to really listen."* You should never insert a word between *"to"* and the verb it modifies, in this case *"listen."* You know, it always bothered me during *Star Trek* episodes when they would say *"to boldly go where no man has gone before."* That's just plain wrong. It should be *"**to go boldly** where no man has gone before."*

Rachel: Focus, Dad! How did we get off onto *Star Trek*? Your not listening to me.

Me: I think you meant to say, *"**You're** not listening to me."* You made the common mistake of confusing the second person possessive with the contraction for *"you are."* It would be proper, for example,

to say *"**your** feelings have been hurt because **you're** convinced that Brad is cheating on you."* Do you understand?

Rachel: No, Dad. Do <u>YOU</u> understand???!!! Did you even hear a word I've been saying? I think Brad is sleeping with my best friend. I think he may be more into her then he is into me. What would you do?

While emailing with my daughter, I discovered some deep-seated problems with which she was grappling, like how she apparently slept through her entire 7th grade grammar class. Poor kid.

Me: You know, Rachel, if you're truly serious about resolving your issues, try perusing the Oxford Dictionary. I will gladly share with

YOU'RE GROUNDED FOR LIFE

you my copy, dog-eared as it is. It will explain more clearly than I can the difference between "then" and "than."

Rachel: Arrrrgggghhh!!! I don't care about the difference between *"thin"* and *"then"*. I'm telling you, Brad is like totally ignoring me for that slut.

Me: Rachel, Rachel, Rachel. We just went through this. It's "than" and "then." Please pay attention.

Rachel: Hello? What planet are you even on????

Me: That would be *"On what planet are you?"* Would you like me to go over the dangling preposition issue one more time? And a single question mark at the end of your sentence should suffice.

Rachel: NO, I DO NOT WANT YOU TO GO OVER THE DANDILION PROSTITUTION ISSUE ONE MORE TIME!!! Do you want to help me or not? Should I dump Brad before he dumps me? I can't stand the thought of him with Brianna. Its starting to effect my schoolwork.

Me: No it's not.

Rachel: How would you freakin' know if its effecting my schoolwork or not?

Me: Because the word you're looking for is *"affecting."* *"Effect"* is a noun. And it should be *"it's,"* not *"its"* because *"its"* is the possessive of *"it"*, but you were attempting to use it incorrectly as a contraction.

Rachel: That's a **huge** help, Dad. Just the advice I was looking for. I could care less about all this drama! I see now that I made a big mistake.

Me: By *"big mistake,"* I presume you're referring to your use of the phrase *"I could care less"* when you meant *"I **couldn't** care less"*?

Rachel: Yes, Dad. That's exactly the mistake I was talking about. You understand me so well. Sigh. I can't put into words how, um, unexpected, your advice has been. : v (

Me: I'm so pleased. Rachel, it means a lot to me that we had this little chat.

Rachel: Whatever. By, Dad.

Me: Um, that would be *"Bye, Dad."* The word "by" is a preposition meaning near or next to. Love you, sweetie.

I feel I made a genuine connection with my daughter. I'm glad I could be there to help her work through her many problems. She is such a sweet girl. I wonder how things are going for her with her boyfriend, Brad. He seems like such a nice young fellow.

YOU'RE GROUNDED FOR LIFE

My Advice to the Graduating Class: Don't Tweet Your Junk

Greetings to this year's college graduating class. My, don't you all look so grown up in your elegant caps and gowns and iPods blasting out *Death Cab for Cutie* at full volume. It seems only yesterday that you were stumbling around in Huggies and toddler booties and iPods blasting out Raffi at full volume. Every May, Graduation Day arrives for millions of American college seniors like you. As has been my tradition since 1963, this is my annual Advice to the College Graduating Class of whatever year it happens to be when you're reading this.

My advice to you? Don't pay attention to anyone who tries to give you advice...except for the advice I am about to share, of course. It's important that you make your own choices in life. So make good ones. In looking back on the choices I made in my youth, I realize I made some poor ones now and then. If I had it to do over again, I wish I hadn't taken three years of **Latin** in high school. I'm not Catholic so becoming Pope is probably out of the question. So exactly when would I ever have used it? Never.

I also should never have taken *Post-Modern Latvian Studies* in college. That *[#bleep#]-ing* bastard Professor Yuri Švābe was a cruel son of a bitch. I wish he would die a painful, wrenching death for totally messing up my GPA.... I mean, er, um, I found him to be rather draconian in his grading methodology. Perhaps most of all, I deeply regret rooming with Tony Markowitz of Monmouth, New Jersey for two years in college. Not only was he a complete slob and never did the dishes, but he always smelled like bass and routinely ate my Lucky Charms without asking. I urge you to learn from my youthful mistakes.

For many people, a college education is an important prerequisite to a financially rewarding and meaningful career. Take me, for example. I was fortunate enough to make it into a *nationally ranked* school, University of Virginia (it ranked #1 in Lacrosse last year). I earned mostly good grades and followed that up with two post-graduate degrees (*Advanced Post-Modern Latvian Studies* and *Super-Advanced Ultra Post-Modern Latvian Studies*). And as a result of all my hard work and dedication, years later, I have this humor blog to show for all my effort. Okay, perhaps, that's not actually helping me drive home the importance of a college education.

Since I am proficient in Latin, I decided to look up the etymology of the word "graduate." You may be surprised to learn that it comes from *"gradus"* meaning *"**step**"* and *"u-ate"* which is the past tense of *"**u eat**"*. So it literally means *"steps having been eaten by you"* or more simply put, *"you ate steps."* Guess that third year of Latin paid off after all.

As you transition into the next chapter of your life (known as *un-employment*) set your goals high. Don't let others tell you what you're capable of. On the Internet Highway of Life, don't settle for "basic cable." Go for the platinum plan, with 400 channels, the one with India's All-Access Mumbai Cricket League and the Cambridge University Chess Channel.

Time for some positive self-talk. Look in the mirror and remind yourself that YOU are precisely what employers are looking for right now in this wide open job market: a low-achieving, drunken college graduate with no experience, no motivation and no discernible skills other than being the proud owner of the high score in **Halo 3** in your fraternity house three years running. You deserve that $80,000/year job—don't forget the stock options. Employers should be lining up to snag someone of your talents and ambition. But first, get back to the second half of your Madden NFL Football game against Jeremy on the X-Box. You're only down by a touchdown, and your graduation ceremony is not for another 45 minutes.

First, a word to those of you who finished in the top 15% of your class: The rest of you, just skip down a couple paragraphs and we'll catch up in a bit.

Hey, top 15% students! Nice job compiling a 3.8 GPA. Look at you, studying in the stacks until the library closes at midnight.

YOU'RE GROUNDED FOR LIFE

Nice job on your senior thesis about class and religious warfare in Northern Waziristan. You have nothing to worry about from those other turkeys below who hopefully are not reading this section. Most of you will go to a top flight grad school so you don't actually have to look for a boring entry-level job next year like those other boneheads. Be sure to suck up to mom and dad big time and you might get them to pony up another 50 Grand for that MBA program at Wharton. Remember, Father's Day is next month. Take Dad out for golf. Let him win. Compliment his putting game *before* you mention grad school.

Now a private word for the vast majority of you who finished in the middle of the pack: **Moo.** Hello, members of the herd. Okay so you only finished college with a GPA somewhere between 2.6 and 3.4. You didn't exactly hit the ball out of the park. But you didn't strike out looking either. At least it's not like you're one of those losers in the next paragraph. You can be anything you want to be, so long as what you want to be involves looking for a job for the next 10 months and then settling for an entry level clerical position in a 6' x 6' cubicle and a title of "Administrative Assistant" or "Mailroom Specialist" that pays $8.25 an hour. Still you probably could make it into a second rate grad school to pursue a master's degree in **Ancient Greek Metallurgical Techniques.** Yeah, that will open up a lot of doors. Good thinking, Einstein.

And finally, a very special word for you brainiacs who finished in the bottom 15%. Your parents must be so proud. So what if you finished school with a 1.9 GPA and your only academic achievement was that you completed your computer science term paper on time despite being totally hung over. Can't believe your statistics professor gave you only a D- on your field research project: *"Las Vegas Field Study: The Effects of Alcohol on the Probability of Winning at Black Jack."*

Oh, and nice move signing up for all those courses that grade based solely on group projects. It's not like you didn't contribute to the team. Someone had to make those beer runs. Cynics might tell you your job prospects look dim. Don't believe them. The world ahead of you is bursting with opportunity. Of course, when I say *"bursting with opportunity"* what I mean is any job that involves asking people if they'd *"like fries with that"* or you're particularly handy with a forklift. Take comfort in the knowledge that there are thousands of parents all over the world every bit as disappointed in their offspring as yours are.

Graduation day is your big day to bask in the sun—the crowning achievement of your illustrious college career. Hopefully your hangover from last night's toga party won't prevent you from making it to your graduation ceremony before your name is called. Let me give you some helpful advice to make sure your big day goes smoothly: First, if you resume consciousness in time, change out of your toga and slip into something a bit more 21st century. For guys, pants would be nice. Watch your step as you shuffle inebriatedly to the podium to accept your diploma. That third step to the stage can be tricky.

When you receive your diploma, don't thrust the University Chancellor on top of the podium, hold her in your arms and shout at the top of your lungs *"I'm King of the World."* You're not Leonardo DiCaprio. She's not Kate Winslet. Finally, when you walk off the stage, don't flip the bird to Professor Yuri Švābe and don't shout *"And you thought you could stop me from graduating, you son of a bitch."* I can't emphasize this point enough.

In closing, as you think about your future, remember to lead your life with integrity. Follow your passion. Set your own course. Don't let others tell you what to do or who to be. Live a life of compassion for others. Make the world a better place for those around you and for those who come after you. Ah, who am I kidding? Let some other sap save the world and feed the homeless. Your success in life can be measured by the square footage of your vacation home and the value of your 401K portfolio.

Here's a simple test: If by age 27 you're living in a high rise flat in the financial district of Geneva, Switzerland, you're probably a success. If, on the other hand, at age 27 you're still living at home with mom and dad in the bedroom you grew up in and you

still have that *Dirty Dancing* movie poster on your wall, and if your model of the Star Trek Enterprise you assembled in 8th grade using LEGOs is still on display next to your lava lamp, you're almost certainly a failure. Any questions?

In conclusion, let me leave you with this inspirational quote from my high school Latin teacher, Mr. van den Berg, who once said, and I

Congratulations, college graduates. You could not have picked a better time to enter the job market. I hear they're hiring greeters at Wal-Mart. I'll put in a good word for you.

quote, *"Tutti le verita sono facile da capire, una volte che vengono scoperti, il punto e quello di scoprire loco."* What does it mean? I have no clue. Turns out it's an Italian quote. I don't know Italian, just Latin. So, instead, let me just say, *"Carpe Diem!"* (That's Latin for "seize the carp.") I really have no idea why scholars think this is such a profound concept. Perhaps carp are high in antioxidants.

Memo to Our Kids:
The Family Has Decided to Downsize

[<u>Author's note</u>: The following is a memo I plan to send our daughters when they graduate from college, informing them that they are now officially responsible for their own lives—and phone bills.]

MEMO TO: Junior members of Jones Family Enterprises

FROM: Senior Executive Team

Congratulations to the junior members of Jones Family Enterprises *[henceforth JFE]* on the recent completion of your undergraduate studies. The Senior Executive Team is confident that your long-term economic forecast is bright. We wish we could say the same for your near-term economic outlook. This memo is to inform you of an important decision the executive committee has made regarding your status on the JFE org chart.

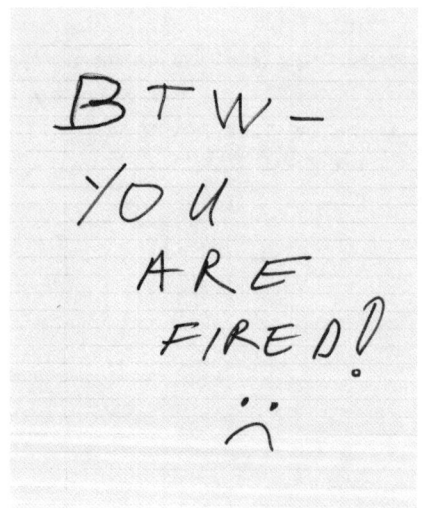

Memo to the junior members of the family business: "It is with regret that we inform you that your services will no longer be required."

After a series of challenging years in which JFE has experienced steadily declining economic growth and spiraling costs, primarily in the area of our educational assistance program, the senior management has decided to implement some immediate cost-cutting measures in order to preserve the organization's long-term cash reserves. This has forced us to make difficult personnel decisions to improve efficiencies and eliminate waste.

Effective immediately, JFE is announcing a 50% reduction in force. As a consequence, we are forced to terminate your roles as

fully-funded dependents of this organization and re-classify your status as "non-essential employees." We considered all other viable options before coming to this decision, including a recommendation by our firm's Co-CEO, Ms. Jones, to eliminate *my* position on the executive steering committee. But that recommendation failed to receive the necessary two-thirds vote required for passage by the two-person executive steering committee.

Please understand that this decision is not personal. It adheres to the terms of our labor contract policies, in which any layoff must apply to those staff members with the fewest years of service. That would be the two of you. After an in-depth review of financial forecasts, the executive committee has concluded that these steps were necessary to protect the solvency of JFE's rapidly diminishing retirement pension plan.

As former dependents, several fully funded employee benefits you have been receiving are hereby terminated, including, but not limited to, the following: cell phone bills, auto insurance premiums, clothing allowance, use of the organization's company cars, and our generous M & E (meals & entertainment) subsidy program during your summer and holiday visits to our headquarters' facility near Seattle. After much debate, it was also decided that our organization's very popular "kids fly home free" travel perk will be discontinued.

The management of JFE is aware that this staffing reduction may come as a disappointment to both of you. We can appreciate that this move could cause short-term economic volatility in your portfolio as you contemplate launching your own start-up ventures. We apologize in advance that our near-term cash flow projections do not permit us to provide you with seed capital as angel investors. Those funds have been previously earmarked for a three-week Caribbean fact-finding study aboard the *Norwegian Oasis of the Seas.*

We would like to formally acknowledge your many valuable contributions to the growth and success of our family organization over these past 22 years. If you would like the organization to return any of your

357 crayon drawings of rainbows and butterflies or your fourth grade research project, *How Baby Kitties Get Borned*, just inform us of the address to which you would like us to ship these items. We will be happy to include in our shipment the 27 boxes of shoes, makeup, and hair care products you left in your former sleeping quarters here at the home office. Please let us know if you'd like us to include in this shipment the box of condoms you hid under your mattress.

As former dependents, you will immediately be able to take advantage of JFE's attractive severance package. We will provide up to five hours of financial planning counseling which will include the following services at no cost to you:

- The ins and outs of balancing a checkbook

- Calculating how much you'll need to earn to afford a three-bedroom apartment in downtown Manhattan

- Learning how to budget—using cost estimates based on reality and not an episode of *The Bachelor*

- The secrets to writing an employment cover letter using complete words, punctuation, and no emoticons

Our generous severance package also includes an 8 x 10 framed photo of the organization's founding partners. We will throw in a copy of the handy young adult's survival guide, *Twenty-One and Downsized—How to Survive on Your Own Now That Your Free Ride Is Over*, at no extra cost. Helpful chapters include:

- When your parents say *"No, I absolutely will **NOT** pay for that"*, what do they mean?

- Making your own bed—a five-step overview

- Busting the myth that money grows on trees

- Food or Italian designer shoes?—Making the right choice

- Ten reasons why your parents won't pay for grad school

- Five warning signs your roommate is stealing your food

- Wardrobe makeover: How to switch from shopping at Hollister to Target without your friends finding out

We wish you all the best in your future endeavors. Drop us a note with your contact information once you have found gainful employment.

By the way, we anticipate that you may wish to inquire about our "post-college live at home" internship program. You are welcome to apply for this residency program by visiting our website www. NoFreeLunch.com, completing the application form and sending in the non-refundable $250 processing fee. A member of our senior staff will get back to you with our decision in approximately six to eight months.

We invite you to email any questions you have about this reduction in force to dad@notmyproblemanymore.com. Or you can call us anytime (during normal human waking hours) using your own pre-paid cell phone plan.

Sincerely,

Tim Jones
Co-Chief Executive Officer

CHAPTER FOUR

In Case You Haven't Learned by Now, Parenting is Futile

"I wish I could sue any number of people
for this 'Joy of Mothering' scam ...
but you're my son ... and you're taking the fall."

If You're Not a Chinese Tiger Mom, Your Kids Will End Up in Prison

If you're like most parents, every now and then you probably wonder quietly to yourself *"Am I a failure as a parent?"* In the case of Howard Ryerson of Danville, VA, I hate to break it to you, but the answer is *Yes, Howard, you are.*

For the rest of you out there, let's find out just how good a parent you are by taking this amazingly accurate scientifically proven assessment of your parenting effectiveness.

Q1: Are you a parent?

Q2: Do you live in either the United States or Canada?

Q3: Are you Caucasian?

If you answered YES to all three of the above, then statistically speaking, you are almost certainly a TERRIBLE PARENT. In a few years your kids will most likely take a job asking people if they would like to *Super-Size* it for 25 cents more. That's the conclusion (I draw) from Amy Chua's controversial best-selling book, *Battle Hymn of the Tiger Mother.*

In case you've been without electricity for the past eight years—perhaps you were rafting down the Amazon in search of a lost tribe—and you've never heard of this author or her book, let me be the first to welcome you back to Civilization. We've missed you. That's Amy Chua pictured in the photo, carrying her younger child, Lulu, into the jungle, where she will leave her for three days to fend for herself after failing to get 100% on her 8th grade science quiz.

Author Amy Chua and her daughter Lulu.

Chua is a second generation Chinese American and a highly successful Yale law professor. She recently wrote a book about how she has raised her two daughters in the traditional Chinese way. A media firestorm surrounds her book because of the controversial, draconian lengths she has gone to ensure her kids are perfectionist over-achievers—the way she and millions of other Chinese people who will eventually take over this country and become your boss were raised by their parents.

Chua calls her relentless parenting approach the way of the Tiger Mother. This parenting style—common throughout much of China—combines endless rote repetition and memorization of interminably boring drills with harsh discipline, chronic parental disapproval and deprivation of any form of happiness—until the child reaches say, age 27. So naturally, parents all over America are thrilled about this approach.

At first, however, some Western parents might be shocked by some of Chua's extreme parenting techniques—including the now famous story of how she forced her seven-year old daughter Lulu to practice her violin for hours into the night with no food or bathroom breaks, until Lulu performed the piece perfectly. Chua once tore up handwritten birthday cards from her young kids and told them to start over because they hadn't tried hard enough. In her book Chua recalls from her own childhood a time when she received an award for second prize. Her father was enraged, telling her *"Never, ever disgrace me like that again."* (True.)

I read Chua's book and have become an ardent convert to the Tiger Mother approach. Let's face it. Most American parents coddle their kids and praise them for the lamest achievement: *"Great soccer game, Billy. You only gave up 7 goals today. As long as you had fun, that's all that matters. I'm sooooo proud of you!"* Even more embarrassing when you consider Billy is 37 years old and married. In China parents tend to set the bar much higher than we do here in the USA, internalizing an expectation of performance excellence that begins about the time their two-month old has discovered his thumb.

In America, we've lost our competitive edge. If we are going to compete in the 21st century, we need to be more like the Chinese. Chua would argue—and I agree—that in the USA we've raised a nation of soft, spoiled, wimpy children by pampering them with such luxuries as meals every single day, comfortable shoes, and even their own bed to sleep in at night—not to mention clothing that they don't even have to sew themselves. No wonder ours is a nation of over-indulged kids with a sense of entitlement. Everything is handed to them. If you ask me, there's nothing like a 14-hour day in a coal mine to teach your youngster the importance of self-discipline and responsibility. Ah, the good old days.

Most of you know that I am widely considered to be a parenting expert (thanks in part to a chronic string of tragic parenting failures during the first 18 years of my kids' early development). I happen to be the adoptive father of two Chinese daughters, which makes me an expert on the subject of Chinese Tiger parenting.

I realize now that as the father of two Chinese children, I had a moral obligation to raise them applying the strict disciplinarian tactics of their biological ancestors back in the Middle Kingdom. I should never have introduced my Chinese daughters to such frivolous distractions like computers or dolls until they had at proven their worth as Valedictorian of their middle school. Sadly, it's too late for my kids. The Chinese Dragon is out of the barn. My daughters, please forgive me for not depriving you enough during your formative years.

I want to let you in on a little secret: *You don't actually have to be Chinese to be a good parent* (although it helps). If you're white or black, or even Hispanic, over time, you too can eventually become a good parent—*IF* you follow my proven **Six-Step System**. Before you know it, your kids will be calling you Tiger Mom (or Dad)—not to mention a few other creative words they may add to their vocabulary when describing their new feelings about their parents.

Get started today, and you can pretty much mail your child's acceptance letter to Harvard in a couple months—unless, of course, she had her heart set on Oxford.

[The fine print: In a small number of cases, my Six-Step Tiger Mother system may result in a lifetime of emotional scarring to your child's psyche. In rare cases offspring may sever all communication with their parents for the rest of their lives. This approach may result in serious cases of parental or child depression, emotional exhaustion, or chronic shouting matches over why your child is not allowed to have any friends over. Do not try this approach if you want to have any relationship with your child in the years ahead. Your mileage may vary. Not recommended for anyone living in Vermont. Do not try this if your child's first name begins with the letter C.]

Step 1: Become Chinese. Admittedly, for some of you, like my fair-skinned, red-headed wife of Canadian-Scottish ancestry, this could be a bit of a stretch at first. But trust me, becoming Chinese will make the remaining steps much easier. If you can't become Chinese, then at least shoot for becoming Vietnamese, or perhaps Indonesian. At least make an effort. Start by practicing smiling uncomfortably and bowing a lot. Sell your Ford Fusion and start riding a bicycle everywhere. View anyone from Japan with suspicion.

Step 2: Enforce a policy of ZERO TOLERANCE for first time offenses. Whether it be failing to do their homework or not making their bed, in the world of the Tiger Mother, there are no second chances. First offense: Instant grounding for a week. Second offense: No college for you, little lady. Third offense: You are no longer a member of this family. Please leave now. And remember, when it comes to kids rudely talking back to their parents, one Taser is worth a thousand words.

Step 3: Insist on a Juilliard School of Music mastery of their choice of instrument (permissible options include violin, cello or piano). Say that it's your seven-year old Luke's birthday today, but he has still not mastered *Rachmaninoff's Piano Concerto No. 3*. No worries. Just tell him to keep practicing until he gets it perfect.

Inform Luke that you can always celebrate his birthday next year, and then donate his birthday presents to charity. I'm sure the local Humane Society needs a Play Station 3.

The next time he whines that he has been practicing for four hours nonstop and he's tired and wants to go to bed, remind him that *"Sleep is for winners, not losers, like you."* For starters, watch the inspiring family film, *Glengarry Glen Ross*. Remember, little boy, Cookies are for Closers.

Step 4: Establish a clear set of academic achievement standards. No more *A's for Effort*. No more consoling your child when he gets a B+ on his science paper with phrases like *"I'm sure you did your best."* Don't settle for anything less than 2300 on their SAT's (out of a possible 2400). And that's if they're in 5th grade. Once they reach high school, their SAT scores better surpass 2400.

Parents of high school seniors, remind your child that anything less than Valedictorian means paying for college on their own, thanks to the shame they've brought on the family. Don't wait too long to get started. We recommend beginning no later than month five of your pregnancy if you want your child to stand any chance of beating out the competition. The Changs next door started in month three. And their girl, Fiona, now eleven, just got accepted to Berkeley. Better get a move on.

Step 5: Be quick to withhold affection and approval for the slightest shortcomings. Too often kids fall short of their potential because they weren't pushed enough. Look at me. I write a humor blog. Need I say more? Parents often make the mistake of telling their kids how proud they are of them - *no matter what.* You probably hug your kids and remind them every day how much you love them, don't you? How could you be so cruel? You barbarian!

I tell you, nothing like some seriously ***conditional*** love to snap your kids into action. Remind them every day that caring parents like you simply cannot give their love to a child who obviously mailed it in and got a mere A- in Algebra II. Make sure your child understands that unless she makes first string on the Girls' Varsity

YOU'RE GROUNDED FOR LIFE

Soccer team, you will have no choice but to update your will to give her portion to her younger brother. Can't spell "hippopotamus"? No bedtime story for you, Benny. You can never remind your child enough just how much of a bitter disappointment they have been. It builds character. They will thank you for your tough love (albeit perhaps 30 years after you've passed away).

Step 6: Avoid any activities that could expose them to fun. Having fun means your kids are wasting time when they should be working on their physics term paper or discovering a new element for the Periodic Table. Hanging around with neighborhood kids will only delay their cognitive development and prevent them from obtaining that $175,000/year

Child of a Tiger Mother staring out her living room window at a Good Humor truck, wondering what an ice cream sandwich tastes like.

entry level position at Johns Hopkins when they graduate from Princeton. *[Note: Harvard, Yale, MIT and Stanford are also acceptable institutions. University of Florida? Don't insult me.]*

You see, we Tiger parents know that "Fun" is nothing more than a euphemism for "**Failure**." Be sure to protect your impressionable young children from destructive distractions like sleep-overs, music (other than classical), birthday parties, Sponge Bob Square Pants or anything with the name **Disney**. Never let them near a computer until they have reached 18 unless it's to finish their research paper conclusively disproving Newton's Law of Universal Gravitation—for which they had better get an A or else someone is sleeping in the pup tent for a week.

Longitudinal clinical studies show that if you apply my proven Six-Step Tiger Mothering system, there is a 20% chance your youngster will grow up to become an extraordinarily highly successful standout in their chosen field. *[Note: Acceptable chosen fields*

include Head of Research at GlaxoSmithKline, Chief of Surgery at the Mayo Clinic, and Attorney General for the State of Massachusetts or First Violinist for the New York Philharmonic.] Do not be confused by the studies' footnote findings that indicate a remote (45%) chance your child could grow up to hate their parents, become a psychotic serial killer and turn to a life of drugs to ease the pain of their cruel, bleak existence chasing after their parents' dreams.

Good luck as you embark on your new role as a Tiger Parent. You'll thank me later. I have to wrap this up. I need to waterboard my youngest. Seems like someone forgot to brush her teeth after breakfast again.

YOU'RE GROUNDED FOR LIFE

What We WISH We Could Say to Our Kids

Years ago, I had this reckless notion that something was missing in my life that could only be filled by having kids. So we started a family—and got so much more: eight years of Raffi songs, 800 trips to sports practices (and the occasional trip to the ER), $6,000 in orthodontia bills, and a child-proofed house, every square inch of which perpetually resembled a FEMA disaster zone.

Don't get me wrong—I love our daughters more than anything in the world—with the possible exception of bacon. But it didn't take long to discover that despite the significant gap between my toddlers and me in earning potential, overall intelligence, and ability not to drool on everything, I simply was no match for my kids. They routinely wore me out—usually by the time they dumped a bowl of Raisin Bran on each other—a daily 7am ritual.

As a parent of two boisterous young girls, I quickly came to two conclusions: First, the interior of the VCR makes an ideal place to hide daddy's slice of apple pie; and second, being a parent was going to require Herculean levels of patience. Being a good parent means having the maturity to resist saying the first thing that pops into your prefrontal cortex when your eight-year-old microwaves your cell phone. You need to suppress the urge to blurt out, *"Jesus Christ! What the hell were you thinking, spraying the cat with purple paint, you little twerp?"* Such an outburst could permanently damage your precious child's delicate self-esteem—much like permanent marker can permanently damage our precious leather couch.

Shortly after our girls acquired rudimentary speech, I learned a valuable lesson: Never use foul language in front of young children. When my eldest was barely three, I caught her wielding my brand new Titleist driver into the trunk of our cherry tree, *"Just like George Washington, Daddy!"* While she hadn't yet mastered conjugating a sentence, she had, to my surprise, absolutely no difficulty reciting back to mommy the entirety of my panicked outburst—verbatim: *"Mommy, Daddy said, 'Holy shit. Look what you've done to my club!' What does 'shit' mean, Mommy?"*

If you're considering starting a family, my best advice is to discuss it with friends who have already chosen that path—and seriously re-think your impulsive decision. Why not pursue a far less expensive endeavor, like, say, purchasing your own Lear jet? But if you won't listen to reason, then at least practice what you plan to say to your child before they begin their devious campaign to drive you insane. Let me help with a few suggestions:

When your five-year-old explodes into a full-blown tantrum be-cause you won't let him have chocolate chip cookie dough for dinner ...

Consider saying this: *"If you stop screaming and let go of your sister's hair, then we will calmly discuss your proposal. Now eat your meatloaf and peas or else you can go to your room now without dinner."*

Even though what you really want to say is this: *"Well, ex-cuse me, your majesty. I had no idea that you had called for the chef to prepare your usual en-trée of refined sugar and corn*

Looks like it's going to be a major task cleaning up this mess. Don't fret - it could've been much worse. He did this Sharpie masterpiece at your boss' house – it could have been your place. Phew.

syrup. Please forgive the egregious error. I will have the chef sum-marily beheaded at dawn. Would you like some whipped cream and gummy bears as well? And what festive melody would you like the minstrel to play on his lute for his majesty's amusement? I live to serve your every whim, sire."

When your eight-year-old asks you, *"Daddy, how come the moon doesn't fall out of the sky?"*, and no matter how many times you try to explain gravity and planetary physics, he keeps asking the same question over and over again for the next hour ...

Consider saying this [to your spouse]: *"So, honey, how was your day?"*

YOU'RE GROUNDED FOR LIFE

Even though what you really want to say is this [to your child]: *"If you ask me 'how come the moon doesn't fall out of the sky' one more time, I swear I am going to send you to the frickin' moon on the next one-way space ship, where they will drop you off and you can ask the goddamned man on the moon yourself. But you might want to bring a sweater, bucko—since it's minus 387 Fahrenheit there—Now just shut your pie hole, for once in your life."*

When you come home two hours earlier than planned and find your fifteen-year-old hosting a kegger for fifty of his closest pre-pubescent friends...

Consider saying this: *"I am deeply disappointed in you. There will be serious consequences for this violation of my trust. I need to sleep on it tonight so I can decide on the appropriate punishment. In the meantime, clean up this mess you made right now."*

Even though what you really want to say is this: *"What the hell were you thinking? Oh right, you WEREN'T thinking. Because you're an idiot! What exactly was your plan, Sherlock—setting up a keg and inviting strippers to jump out of a cake? Here's a suggestion: The next time you decide to throw a beer party for your underage friends in my house, make sure to change the lock on the front door. That way, it will buy you just enough time to make your escape out the back and hop on a bus to Mexico before I break down the door and shove that keg up your ass and out your ear. FYI, you're grounded until the return of Haley's Comet."*

So if you're still contemplating starting a family, see what you have to look forward to? But honestly, give my suggestion about buying a Lear jet instead serious consideration. It is way cheaper in the long run.

Better Parenting Though Polling

When it comes to parenting, I don't always make the best decisions. I'm not always sure what the right thing to do is in a difficult situation.

Like the time our elder daughter begged and pleaded with me to let her drive the car to the mall. It was a sunny day. Traffic was light. And she had behaved extremely well all week long. So against my better judgment, I said okay. Two minutes later, she smashed the car into a stop sign barely 100 yards

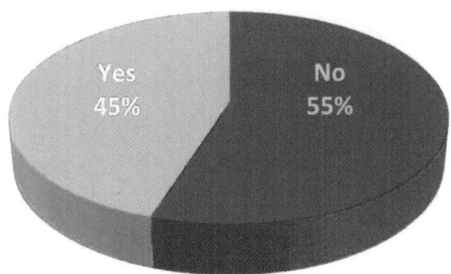

The latest parenting poll: Should I pay for my kid's college or buy myself that new Mustang? 55% of midlife crisis dads polled say, "Buy the car."

from our driveway. A part of me can't help but wonder whether in retrospect I made a mistake giving in to the incessant pleadings of an eight-year-old to drive my minivan.

Sometimes my wife questions my ability to make the right call. Heck, she rarely listens to any of my opinions unless at least four complete strangers tell her the exact same thing—which got me to thinking: maybe the way for me to make better parenting decisions is to poll the opinions of total strangers.

In the 2012 presidential election, the polls were incredibly accurate forecasters of people's voting preferences. Nate Silver's 538 blog accurately predicted the Electoral College winner in all fifty states. Politicians use polls all the time to help them decide how to vote. Should we legalize gay marriage? Poll your constituents. Should we cut defense spending? Do a poll. Should we ban hurricanes during the last week of a presidential campaign? (97% of Republicans resoundingly voted yes.)

YOU'RE GROUNDED FOR LIFE

I figure, maybe I can learn a thing or two from those politicians. That's why I've decided to stop listening to my inner voice when confronted by a difficult parenting issue. Now I make all my important parenting decisions by means of polling. I have benefitted from the collective wisdom of a much broader community in many matters:

Poll Question #1: What punishment is appropriate for our elder daughter, who missed curfew for the third time in two weeks, giving the lame excuse that she missed the last bus from the library and had to walk the six miles home? According to my poll of **328 Boston Red Sox season ticket holders**:

- 59% said that I should give her some slack since, after all, she *was* studying at the library.

- 24% said I should talk with her and ask her what she thinks the consequences should be.

- 9% said she's had plenty of warnings and I should ground her until spring training.

- 8% said I should put in a pinch hitter and attempt a bunt to move the runner on second over to third.

Poll Question #2: The last time our younger daughter cleaned up her room, Scott Walker was leading in the Republican race for president. Her room now looks like a home in the wake of Hurricane Sandy. What should I do? I polled **147 Guatemalan goat herders** and here's how they weighed in on the matter:

- 37% said that unless it presents a safety issue, I should just let it go. Pick my battles.

- 29% said a sloppy room is a sign of disrespect for the head of the household. She should be punished by having to sleep outside with the goats in their pen for 20 nights.

- 34% said "What is a Scott Walker?"

- 100% said, "Your daughter has her own room?"

Poll Question #3: Our two teenage daughters squabble all the time. Lately their arguments have escalated into nasty name-calling with curse words and profanity. What should I do about this the next time they start after each other? I polled **275 Amish families in Lancaster, PA**, and here is how they responded:

Concerning the proper punishment for my daughter's D on a test, the third grade class of Duncan Creek Elementary overwhelmingly voted *Give her lots of candy.* **Experts question the statistical validity of the sample.**

- 39% said that this is typical teenage behavior and I should not intervene. Let them sort it out.

- 28% said take away all their consumer electronic devices for a week. The Amish have lived without cell phones for years; the girls can survive without theirs for a week.

- 18% said that the girls' use of curse words is an affront to God. Teach them a lesson in cooperation by making them build a barn together—no power tools allowed.

- 15% said when they're done building the barn, they can start working on the grain silo. It's in serious need of repairs. And while they're at it, it wouldn't kill them to repaint the school.

After the Amish voted, they discussed the issue further. To my surprise, they all changed their minds—and unanimously voted for shunning.

YOU'RE GROUNDED FOR LIFE

Using this polling system has dramatically reduced my stress level. I can't actually say it's helped me arrive at any better parenting decisions, but at least now I can point the blame somewhere else. Next time my wife gets on my case about a bad parenting call and screeches, "Who in the world thought it was a good idea to let our daughter have a pet llama?" My response is simple: "A focus group of Peruvian llama ranchers, honey."

In a few cases, however, the feedback has been perplexing. I polled a group of Tea Party activists about how to discuss the dangers of drinking and driving with my college-age daughter. 87% of respondents said the critical thing I need to do is to lower taxes, repeal Obamacare, and get the federal government out of my life. I'm not really sure what this has to do with the dangers of drinking and driving. Maybe if I dress up as George Washington it will make more sense to me.

My wife is not on board yet with my new parenting approach. She is old-fashioned. Amusingly, she still thinks the best approach is to stay calm, be clear in our expectations and apply logical consequences for our children's poor choices. Sounds like way too much work, if you ask me.

Frankly, I'm not so sure my wife's outdated parenting methodology works any better than my new system. So I polled 195 soccer dads about which approach they feel is more effective, mine or hers. They were divided on the question. But there was an overwhelming consensus on a related issue: They all agreed the coach does not give their kid nearly enough playing time.

Nine Things I Wish I Hadn't Worried About So Much as a Parent

As a parent, you never stop worrying about your kids or how they will turn out. Will they grow up safe? Will they make good choices? Will they ever forgive you for buying them those matching green and orange plaid square dance dresses for their 13th and 14th birthdays?

The other day, I reflected on all the things I've worried about as a parent. I came to a startling realization: I spent much of the past 20 years needlessly worrying—fretting over how to be a better parent, be a positive role model, and keep my kids from making poor choices. In retrospect, I needn't have been so anxious. I was never going to get it right. I finally realized that my kids were going to make it through this bumpy journey called childhood moderately unscathed, regardless of my egregious parenting mistakes. In retrospect, I should have spent a lot less time worrying about whether they brushed their teeth and a lot more time about worrying how to cure my slice in golf. Then again, trying to cure my golf slice is about as futile as trying to be the perfect parent. Both end up in bitter disappointment.

Here are nine parenting lessons I wish I hadn't worried about nearly so much over the past 20 years:

Lesson One: Share your toys. This message never quite sank in. Just last week, I heard Rachel shouting at Emily: "*Stay out of my room. If you touch my computer, you'll pay.*" Seems the concept of sharing your toys is still as enigmatic for my daughters as the concept of String Theory in quantum physics. Apparently the act of simply touching any possession—a dress, earrings, hair brush, or lip gloss—by the opposing sister makes the aforementioned item toxically infected and irreparably damaged, and constitutes legitimate grounds for full scale retaliation—usually involving the misappropriation of the enemy sibling's high school sweatshirt, favorite shoes and Johnny Depp poster.

YOU'RE GROUNDED FOR LIFE

Lesson Two: Don't eat junk food. Here's another life message that didn't quite take hold. Despite constant conversations about the risk of childhood obesity, heart disease, and the probability that their brain would dissolve into a wad of chocolate chip cookie dough, our girls never quite internalized the importance of healthy eating. Fortunately so far at least, neither is overweight—which may explain why my constant harping about proper nutrition never really resonated. Or perhaps it was the fact that I usually still had frosting from a Krispy Kreme glazed donut on my chin during my lecture.

Lesson Three: Don't watch so much junk television. They say the average American toddler spends more than 32 hours per week watching television. I'm proud to say our two kids have done their part to keep these averages up. My girls have watched just about every episode of *America's Next Top Model* since 2007. As a result, I am confident they are now ready for the challenges of adulthood—just so long as those challenges require sultry strutting down a catwalk in 5-inch heels and photo shoots dressed as a lioness, purring provocatively on the hood of a Lamborghini.

Like many concerns of the moment, my worries about watching too much junk TV eventually faded away, as my girls began to waste less time mindlessly watching the boob tube. Now they spend these hours doing something much more constructive: mindlessly sending thought-provoking texts like *"What's up? #HAHA!"* to their 947 closest friends—as they typically do the moment they arrive home and make glancing eye contact with one of their parents.

Lesson Four: Do your chores. Yet another parental lecture that seems to have made no impression was my weekly sermon about how we all share the responsibility to keep our home tidy and clean. I came up with all sorts of strategies and rewards to incentivize them for doing their chores on time. But none of them worked. And lest you think I was a push-over and simply let them get away with not doing their part, I put my foot down. *"Do your chores or it's no TV for you!"* Oh sure, technically speaking, they still didn't do their chores most of the time. But they didn't get to watch any TV either. They had to watch their shows over the Internet on their laptop's small screen. That'll teach 'em.

Lesson Five: Be polite to your sister. For years, our girls used to constantly antagonize each other over the slightest transgression.

I am convinced the primary objective was just to piss off their sibling. No issue was too trivial to draw the line in the sand and declare war: Which Disney TV show they were going to watch, who should get the last cookie, or more recently, how *"everybody at school knows your boyfriend is totally into Madison over you."*

Birthday cake is the great mediator to bring together fighting siblings. Silent bliss to the last bite. Then all hell breaks loose.

I am pleased to report that after almost two decades of lecturing, cajoling, pleading and periodically blackmailing our kids about the importance of being polite to their sister, I have made modest progress. Recently, Emily asked Rachel to pass the salt at dinner, and Rachel said, *"Get it yourself. I mean, get it yourself,* ***please.****"* This past summer, there was actually a period of two hours where the girls were in the same room as each other and not a single unkind word was spoken. Okay, so Rachel was taking a nap at the time, but that's not the point. The point is they were not picking on each other for two whole hours. What silent bliss! I am hopeful that it's just a matter of time before they get past their differences and become BFFs. Probably about ten years after I'm gone. Much like Don Quixote, I cling to this impossible dream.

Lesson Six: Put your toys away after you use them. I thought it was a pretty simple concept: The toys go back in the toy box. The dirty dishes go in the dish washer. Put your used bath towel back on the towel rack. But apparently the process is far more complicated than I ever realized because 15 years later, my daily

YOU'RE GROUNDED FOR LIFE

message still appears to be as undecipherable to my teenage girls as ancient Egyptian hieroglyphics.

Whenever I've said *"Please hang your coat in the closet,"* somewhere between the time the words leave my mouth and enter their inner ear, the audio waves somehow morph into *"please don't hang up your coat. I want to remember it lying there, in the middle of the kitchen table, on top of your dirty gym clothes, forever." The* typical response I get to any request to put an item away is always the same: *"Yeah, I know"*—which I now am convinced translates loosely as *"over my dead body."*

Lesson Seven: Practice your piano. While we suspected that neither girl was destined for a career as a concert pianist with the New York Philharmonic, still, it would have been nice if they had actually gone through the motions of trying to practice now and then. Between the two of them we went through six years of piano lessons. I'm pretty sure they both mastered *Twinkle, Twinkle, Little Star.*

It was worth the thousands of dollars we poured down the draier, invested in their music education, just to hear them plink out something that sounded vaguely like *Jingle Bells* at the annual Holiday recital. Sure, their performances were rough around the edges, but sitting through 37 other kids' interpretations of Jingle Bells over the course of 5 hours, when I could have been home eating pizza, watching the Seahawks football game, was worth it for the watered down punch and stale cookies they provided afterward.

Lesson Eight: Dress modestly. At about 12 years of age, our girls entered into that magical, mysterious stage known as puberty— when over the course of 18 months, much like a caterpillar morphs into a lovely butterfly, our precious little bundles of joy morphed into cauldrons of raging hormonally charged drama queens who looked amazingly like our former daughters. Of course, eventually they emerged out the other side as young ladies with their new

bodies. And that's when the lesson of dressing modestly became a weekly, and sometimes daily, soap opera.

Turns out that my Neanderthal parenting notion as to what's appropriate attire is not always shared by my more haute couture teenage daughters. I must be stuck in a 1950s time warp. I thought that dressing like Lady Gaga was not quite appropriate for a 15-year-old girl. Even my wife agreed with me on this parenting topic, so surely I had to be right for once. I have concluded that a parent's level of disapproval of their daughter's fashion choice is directly proportional to the likelihood their daughter will insist that everybody at school is wearing this. Perhaps there once was a time, back in 1957, when it could be said that *Father Knows Best,* but in our household, the way I worry about how teenage girls want to dress these days, it's more like *Sleepless in Seattle.* Which leads me to my final lesson....

When your daughter turns 16, this is the kind of boy she'll want to date. The "bad boy." But don't worry. At least he's wearing pants – up to his butt crack.

Lesson Nine: All teenage boys are evil. For years my daughters agreed with my objective assessment about boys (although they were more likely to say *"boys have cooties"*). But as they became teenagers, my girls became brainwashed by a nefarious toxin called estrogen to view the enemy more sympathetically. As I have long maintained, there is no question that all teenage boys are evil. If you are the parent of teenage boys, I mean no disrespect. I am sure that over time your sons will mature, grow out of this evil phase, and stop hitting on my daughters. They may even become caring, doting fathers of their own evil teenage boys someday. My two daughters seem determined not to heed my loving, highly informed parental counsel on this topic and will no doubt have

to learn the hard lesson that teenage boys are interested in only three things: sex and breasts.

So there you go. I have spent the better part of the past 20 years worrying about teaching these important life lessons to my two daughters. I would say at best I'm batting about .125—on a good day. God blessed us with two wonderful, headstrong, independent daughters who have discovered that human beings reach their maximum wisdom at whatever age they have attained.

They are supremely confident that they have all the answers to life's important questions, like who's hotter, Ryan Gosling or Channing Tatum. I now realize that the dozens of parenting books, lectures, and parenting web sites I have pored over during the past 20 years were completely futile. Our kids were going to do what they were going to do, and become the people they were going to become, regardless of the life lessons I tried to teach.

You want my advice? Relax. Stop stressing over whether you're a good parent or not. The odds are at least 92% that you've failed. And it's way too late to fix things now. But somehow, I suspect they will manage this thing called life just fine anyway. Besides, nothing you do will get your kids to follow your advice anyway. Based on my own longitudinal field studies over the past two decades, my theory is that the primary job responsibility of today's American kids is this: *"Roll your eyes while mom or dad drones on about 'making good choices.' Then do exactly **the opposite** of whatever they tell you to do. If you get caught, blame it on your sister."*

... Wait a minute, I just noticed that my girls are actually sitting on the couch right now—and they're both conscious. And neither one is accusing the other of stealing their blow dryer or being a snot-nosed bi-atch. What's this? They are laughing and joking? They actually seem to be getting along? Oh, my God. I have to get this on video. The wife is never going to believe this.

When it Came to the Journey of Parenthood, I Took a Guilt Trip

I have a confession to make. While technically speaking, I was raised in a Presbyterian household, I am sure that my parents secretly were Catholics. That's because for my entire life, no matter how hard I tried, I never felt my efforts were good enough. I've always felt guilty. Especially when it comes to parenting.

When our two girls were toddlers, I mainly swung between three emotional states: totally overwhelmed, utterly exhausted and constantly feeling guilty. That guilt was usually caused by my feeling so overwhelmed and exhausted. When I became so sleep-deprived that I simply had to take a nap, I felt guilty for napping. I mean, a good dad would surely tough it out and watch a *Sponge Bob* video with the kids—for the 475th time. What kind of dad was I! For shame.

I felt guilty about my job in a dotcom startup where for years I routinely worked 75-hour weeks. For some periods, I was essentially an absentee parent until the weekend arrived. And on those rare occasions when I was able to leave work *before* 6pm, I felt guilty because all the other managers (who were all 15 years younger, single and child-free) would still be there well past 8pm.

I felt guilty that my wife unfairly bore the burden of most of the household chores, not to mention the 4am feedings and diaper-changes. By the time I finally got around to helping out with diaper changes, my girls were seven and six years old. Hey, better late than never, I say!

A few years later, I quit the stressful world of internet startups. I decided to scale back my work hours so I could spend more time with our kids. Then I felt guilty that I was earning about 40% less than before, and as a result, vacations to sunny California were replaced by long weekends camping in rain-soaked tents. I never really liked camping as much as my wife did, which of course, is another thing I felt guilty about.

When I was eventually able to spend more time with my young, impressionable daughters, I felt guilty for raising my voice in frustration too many times. Why couldn't I laugh at their daily attempts to destroy everything of value in our home? Like the time I discovered they had hidden my cheeseburger in the fish tank. Why couldn't I just go with the flow and see the humor when they conducted an impromptu science experiment to test how well hamsters swim...in the toilet...just before they flushed....We miss you, Zippy. God rest your furry little soul.

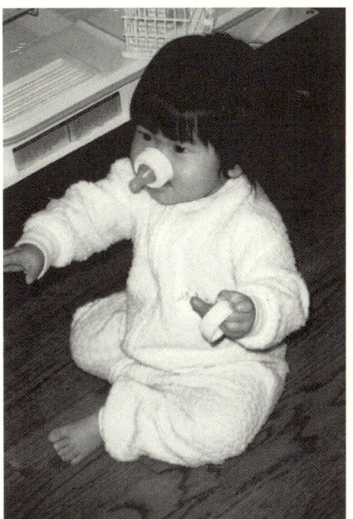

I felt guilty for all the times my *angel monsters*, as I called them back then, had "owies" that I could not make go away. As they grew and their injuries became more serious, I felt guilty that I could not stop the genuine

My wife didn't appreciate my unique approach to weaning Emmy from the bottle. I feel guilty about that. Sigh.

pain of a gushing wound or remove the fear my daughter must have felt being wheeled into the operating room for foot surgery, particularly because it was her arm that was broken.

I felt guilty all the times I said *"No"* to my elder daughter's requests for ice cream on the way home from her soccer games. In retrospect, I probably should not have eaten so many triple-scoop chocolate chip cookie dough ice cream cones in front of her in the car, but what dad can say *"No"* to a chocolate-dipped waffle cone? Not me, that's for sure. Bad dad. I'm a bad dad.

When our girls became teenagers, I felt guilty when I snapped at them for things that most teenagers do, like lying to my face about where they were till 2am in the morning—which in fairness, they only did whenever I would ask them this question. I wish I had not raised my voice in anger when my older daughter totaled the rear end of my new car, along with our garage door, which she failed to notice was still closed because she was busy putting on her lipstick—while driving 20 mph—in reverse. Why didn't I stay calm?

I remember feeling guilty when my younger daughter told me in 11th grade that *"You are the worst dad in the world"* (a direct quote) because apparently she'd concluded she was the only kid whose father had *not* bought their daughter a car for getting a 2.0 average on their report card. I was so mean.

Now that my girls are in college, I feel guilty that I did not cover the complete cost of their college education. My wife and I decided we wanted them to contribute, hoping they might learn a lesson in self-reliance. When they came home from college, I felt guilty when I was mowing the lawn instead of hanging with them, even though I'm pretty sure they both much preferred that I kept mowing the lawn so that I wouldn't ask if they'd like to hang out with me.

Our girls are almost grownups now. And it amazes me how quickly they've transformed from helpless, goop-covered toddlers with poop-filled diapers into self-reliant, self-confident young women intent on charting their own journeys through life. It seems now like it all happened so quickly—barely longer than the time it takes a child to accidentally set the kitchen on fire with her Easy-Bake oven.

As I look back, I feel guilty for having not spent more time with my girls. For not reading them *The Very Hungry Caterpillar* for the umpteenth time. For being unable to wipe away all their innocent tears with the touch of my kiss. For not telling them every single night as I tucked them in that I loved them to the universe and back.

But most of all, I feel guilty that I failed to teach either of my daughters how to throw a football or how to bluff in Texas Hold'em. For that, I am deeply, deeply sorry.

YOU'RE GROUNDED FOR LIFE